Reading
Begins at Birth

David B. Doake

Scholastic

To Diana and Raja,
who shared in the writing of this book
in so many wonderful ways

Scholastic Canada Ltd.
123 Newkirk Road, Richmond Hill, Ontario, Canada L4C 3G5

Scholastic Inc.
730 Broadway, New York, NY 10003, USA

Ashton Scholastic Limited
Private Bag 1, Penrose, Auckland, New Zealand

Ashton Scholastic Pty Limited
PO Box 579, Gosford, NSW, 2250, Australia

Scholastic Publications Ltd.
Holly Walk, Leamington Spa, Warwickshire CV32 4LS, England

Cover photo © John Teasdale/Masterfile
Bil Keane cartoons reprinted by special permission of Cowles Syndicate, Inc.

876543   Printed in Hong Kong   1 2 3 4 5/9

Canadian Cataloguing in Publication Data

Doake, David Brown, 1926-
  Reading begins at birth

(Bright Idea)
Bibliography: p.
ISBN 0-590-71758-8

1. Children - Books and reading. 2. Reading (Preschool).
3. Reading- Parent participation. I. Title. II. Series.

Z1037.A1D62 1988   649'.58   C88-093742-4

Contents

Preface

In a December issue of the journal *Education*, Miss Harriet Iredell had an article published entitled "Eleanor Learns to Read." In it she described how 8-year-old Eleanor, who had never been to school because of her frailness, and who had never been taught at home, was found to be reading fluently. She had been repeating some words to herself, and when asked what she was saying, replied that it was in a book and did they want to hear all of it? Being advised that everyone did, she proceeded to read one of the poems in her book with great expression and obvious enjoyment. Surprised, someone asked, "Who taught you to read, Eleanor?" The child looked puzzled by the question, according to Miss Iredell's report, and her father remarked, "Upon my word, I don't know how she learned to read. But then," he added, "I don't know how she learned to talk either."

Miss Iredell proceeded to reflect on the similarities between oral and written language learning and noted perceptively that:

> Since the two forms of the one mode of expression (language) are so alike in themselves and in their psychological and practical use and effect, it would seem that the principles and rules which govern the acquirement of one must govern the acquirement of the other, and in the natural order of things, they would be learned alike. So much depends upon the truth or falsity of this, that the question claims earnest and immediate consideration.

She continued then to describe, in some detail, how children seem to go through the same natural progression in learning written language as they do in learning oral language, provided similar conditions are present. The year the article was published was 1898!

I wish I could have talked with Miss Harriet Iredell. I am sure I would have learned a lot from her. She was obviously a very astute person who would have been able to give me a great deal of help in my own research into how children learn to read. Almost certainly it would not have taken me so long to arrive at the understandings I now have.

The importance of reading to children has for a long time been seen as a necessary condition for children to learn to read "naturally." In 1908, Edmund Huey stated that a young child could learn to read " . . . as naturally as he learns to speak" and that " . . . the secret of it all lies in the parents reading to and with the child" *(The Pedagogy of Reading)*. Sixty-six years later the U.K. Bullock Commission on Education report stated: "The best way to prepare the very young child for reading is to hold him on your lap and read aloud to him stories he likes to hear, over and over again." Its sensible and sensitive recommendation was to " . . . cradle the child with words."

It sounds too easy, too unscientific, too informal! After all, look how difficult children find learning to read in school when we try to teach them. How can they learn all the rules for "sounding out" words unless they are taught? How can they learn to read accurately unless we constantly listen to them read and correct them when they make mistakes? Surely reading is much too complex a process to be learned so easily!

Yet, for many years, studies of early readers have shown clearly that children can and do learn to read at home without being formally taught. Virtually all of those children, however, grew up in homes of readers and, most significantly, were read to regularly from a very early age. Like Eleanor's father, few of the parents knew their children could read until, like Eleanor, they demonstrated it.

Sceptics have argued that those children all came from "good" homes and were above average in intelligence. Not so, said Dolores Durkin in 1966, referring to her own extensive study of early readers, who came from all ability levels and a variety of home circumstances. Then, it was argued, they must have had a special aptitude, or their parents must have been secretly teaching them at home. In fact, some teachers became quite antagonistic towards the parents if children were already reading when they entered school. They refused to believe the children had not been taught.

For a number of years, I was one of those sceptics. I thought reading was primarily a matter of learning to recognize words — and how can children learn to recognize words unless we teach them? But when I began to look at Marie Clay's studies of early reading development, and Don Holdaway's work with 5-year-old children in inner-city classrooms in Auckland, New Zealand, I began to question my beliefs about how reading is learned.

Both Clay and Holdaway demonstrated that a wide experience with books is a key element in learning to read. Most of Clay's "high progress readers" (children who learn to read quickly and easily on entering school) had come from *literacy-oriented* homes. Holdaway's "shared book experience" approach brought the bedtime story situation into the classroom through the use of enlarged print in various forms, particularly "big books." He showed that even children who came from non-book-oriented homes, and who were learning English as a second language, could become fluent, joyful readers provided they were given regular and extensive experiences with memorable, "predictable" books.

Although the work of these two New Zealanders, and some others, pushed me in a completely new direction, it did not provide me with all the information

I felt I needed to understand fully how children learn to read. What is it that occurs when children are read to on a frequent basis in their homes?

I decided to do what the linguists had done in studying oral language development: go into the homes of preschool children to observe and record. I reasoned that if I observed young children being read to by their parents over a period of time, and noted and tape-recorded everything that happened, I should be able to gain a deeper understanding of how book experiences help make learning to read a natural process. I also wanted to interact with the children myself, with their books and other forms of written language. So I found some willing parents and some unsuspecting children and began my "participant observations." Much of what is in this book is the outcome of that experience.

Some years after I began my studies, my wife Diana and I were blessed by the birth of our son Raja. Since Diana also has a keen interest in reading, and has studied and taught it for many years, some said we had him for "experimental purposes," so we could put our theories to the test! Not so, of course. But we *have* shared books with Raja since the day he was born, not because we wanted to make him into an early reader and so prove that it all works the way we said it did, but because we love books ourselves and knew, with absolute certainty, that his life, and ours, would be enriched by sharing books of all kinds with him. It has been a wonderful experience and we wish we could have it all over again! Raja loves books, loves to be read to and loves reading to himself. We have learned a great deal from him. His experience of growing up immersed in books has enhanced our lives and his. We can recommend the practice with absolute confidence!

I have also been fortunate in other ways. I have found teachers and school principals who have welcomed me into their classrooms to research and continue my investigations of reading and writing. I have seen how positively students of all ages respond to teaching that provides the conditions for them to use their own natural language-learning strategies, instead of spelling out in great detail what they are to learn and when and how. I have also witnessed, over and over again, the devastating effects of literacy instruction based on unnatural language-learning principles.

This book is an attempt to share what I have learned about children — in particular, about how they learn to read. A book can never be a satisfactory substitute for the wonderful insights that result from observing children learning in self-directed ways. It cannot bring the quality of direct experience to its readers. But it can provide an opportunity for those readers to raise additional questions, receive confirmation of what they have been thinking and doing, obtain new understandings, and perhaps gain the confidence to try out new ideas in parenting and teaching. If, as a result of reading this book, a few more parents and a few more teachers help a few more children become avid readers for the rest of their lives, then it will have served its purpose.

I want to express my sincere thanks to the parents of Gillian, Jennifer, Kaaren and Sean, Laura Beth and Adrienne, and, of course, to the children themselves, for inviting me into their homes and providing me with so many special experiences. Acknowledgment must also go to the Social Sciences and Humanities Research Council for their support of the Beginning Literacy Project (S.S.H.R.C. Research Grant No. 410-80-0721R1). Some of the data used were collected as part of that research project.

Prologue: two Lauras

Laura Beth

One day Laura Beth, who was not quite 5 years old, had the following conversation with her mother:

> *Mother:* If you had a little friend who was maybe 4 years old or something like that — say a girlfriend who was 4 years old — and she couldn't read, do you think you could help her learn to read?
>
> *Laura Beth:* Yes, I could help Sandra.
>
> *Mother:* Could you? How could you help Sandra?
>
> *Laura Beth:* Read a book to her lots of times and then she would start to read it and then she would be able to read it and then she could ask her mom to buy it if it's in the store.

Too simplistic? Overly naive? Virtually impossible? Surely this little girl was too young to understand all the complex skills and processes involved in helping someone learn how to read. But then she had been ignorant, too, of all the complex skills and processes involved in learning how to talk, and she had coped with that task with the utmost ease during the first five years of her life. Perhaps what she was saying to her mother does make sense!

Immediately before this conversation, Laura Beth's mother had been recording her attempt to read Margaret Wise Brown's *The Runaway Bunny*. The book had been read to her a number of times and she had decided that she would like to read it to her mother. The story has a simple, highly predictable format. The little bunny says he wants to run away and his mother replies that she will run after him. Each page contains a repeated sequence where the little bunny says he will become something and his mother says she will become someone appropriate to catch him. The following transcript represents how Laura Beth, at the age of 4 years 10 months (4.10), managed the task. She had already read the first seven pages unaided. (Mother's contributions have been recorded in upper case letters. Laura Beth's "miscues" have been underlined.)

Text	Laura Beth
"If you are a gardener and find me,"	"If you (pause) . . . if you (pause again, Mother prompts) . . . ARE a gardener and find me,"
said the little bunny, "I will be a bird and fly away from you."	said the little bunny, "I will be a bird and <u>I</u> (self corrects) — and fly away from you." It says "and fly away

from you." Does that make sense? (Mother: DOES IT?) "And fly away from you . . . and fly away from you."

"If you become a bird and fly away from me," said his mother, "I will be a tree that you come back home to."

"If you be a bird and fly away from me," said his mother, "I will be a tree that you can (repeats) that you can" (pauses) . . . What's that, Mom? (Mother: WHERE? SHOW ME. HOME.) " . . . that you can ho — that you can home to — that you can come home to."

Laura Beth continued to read to the end of the book in this manner, occasionally seeking help from her mother, but mostly working things out for herself. Her reading was fluent and expressive, her involvement in the task exuberant and complete, and her confidence and satisfaction clearly evident in her voice. Laura Beth was teaching herself to read and was obtaining great pleasure from doing so.

The transcript reveals that this not quite 5-year-old girl was well on the way to becoming an independent reader. It is clear that she was using her prior experience with the story to read it for herself, but it is also clear that she was not relying on this alone and was using at least some of the print (visual information) to assist in her reading. Her self-correction of the sentence "I will be a bird and I — and fly away from you" almost certainly would not have been made had she not been using cues available in the print to help her read. She was obviously uncomfortable with the construction " . . . and fly away from you," as indicated by her asking her mother if it made sense, and probably would have completed the sentence with " . . . and I will fly away from you," which sounds more acceptable to her ear and is, in fact, more grammatically correct.

On the next page, she asked her mother for help with the word *home*, but then had trouble fitting it in because of her substitution of "can" for *come*. She quickly resolved that problem, however, when she reconstructed the unacceptable " . . . that you can home to." Not only did she want her story to make sense and sound like language, she also wanted it to be what it looked like on the page.

It is not difficult to understand, then, why Laura Beth viewed the process of learning to read as the outcome of being read to again and again. It is essentially how she learned to read the story of *The Runaway Bunny*. Her mother reported that, at this stage of her development as a reader, her daughter was working her way through an extensive library of familiar and favorite books. She was reading them to herself, to her mother or father, to her dolls, to anyone who would listen.

As she completed each book successfully, she would place it on her dresser in a stack that was growing steadily, day by day. Most significantly, she was reading them by matching very carefully what she was saying with what she was seeing, with her finger and her eyes. As we shall see later, she had reached an extremely important stage in her development as a reader.

Laura Beth was growing up in a literacy-oriented home. She had never received any formal instruction in reading, but had been read to virtually from birth, mostly in the company of her older brother, who had been reading independently from the age of about 3.6 years. She had also demonstrated considerable interest in learning to write and was already composing unsolicited meaningful and readable writing, using her own form of invented spelling. Letters to Father Christmas and the Easter Bunny, messages, notices, greeting cards and written records of various experiences were just some of the forms this writing took. No instruction in writing had been given either, but she had seen a great deal of written language produced in her presence — written language that was functional and relevant. She had been invited to observe its production and had often participated in it. Her approximating efforts had been met with constant praise and encouragement. Her many questions about both reading and writing had been answered clearly and directly and, most important, immediately by parents who knew exactly how to relate new knowledge to what she already knew. Her self-directed literacy learning had been conducted in a warmly supportive and non-corrective atmosphere. She was being given the opportunity to learn to read and write in the same way and at the same time as she was being given the opportunity to learn to talk and listen.

Laura

The other Laura grew up in a very different setting. Diane DeFord (1981) reported the results of an interview she conducted with 7-year-old Laura, who at the time had been in school for two years. Compare how this Laura went about the process of learning to read, and how she would try to help others do so:

Diane: When you're reading and you come to something you don't know, what do you do?

Laura: We sound out the first two letters. After I gots that I try to see another word — if it has three letters.

Diane: Do you ever do anything else?

Laura: If I do all that and I still don't get it, I try my vowel rules.

Diane: Who is a good reader, and what makes them a good reader?

Laura: Rusty, he is a good reader because he always tries the first two letters.

Diane: Do you think he ever comes to something he doesn't know when he's reading?

Laura: Sometimes he misses periods. Even I miss periods sometimes.

Diane: What do you think he does then?

Laura: If it's a word, a real word we aren't used to, he tries the first two letters, or he tries to find a little word.

Diane: If you knew that someone was having difficulty reading, how would you help them?

Laura: I would try to whisper to them to try the first two letters.

Diane: What if that didn't help?

Laura: I would pray that God will help them find the word.

It is doubtful if either her religious education (she was attending a Roman Catholic school) or her reading education was likely to be of much use in her attempts to learn to read — or to help any others do so!

It is not difficult to understand why Laura, age 7, was experiencing considerable frustration in her efforts to learn to read while Laura Beth, age 5, was finding the process easy and enjoyable and was being entirely successful:

- Laura Beth had learned to focus her attention on meaning and language structures, while these crucial aspects clearly had played little part in the kind of instruction Laura had received from her teachers.

- Laura Beth used print cues simply to confirm her predictions, while Laura had been taught to concentrate all her attention on attempting to correctly identify the sounds of the letters. Her teachers had led her away from using her strengths (her knowledge about language and the world around her) and directed her to use meaningless and "languageless" bits and pieces of written language.

- Laura Beth's meaning-oriented strategies would assure her of success, while Laura's, non-meaning-oriented, would almost certainly cause her to experience considerable difficulty in her efforts.

The researcher Heinz Werner stated an important developmental principle related to all aspects of human learning, substantiated through his extensive study (1957):

> . . . whenever development occurs it proceeds from a state of relative globality and lack of differentiation to a state of increasing differentiation, articulation and hierarchic integration (p.126).

Put more simply, we learn best when we first get a feel for the "whole thing" and then start concentrating our attention on the bits and pieces.

Some years later, the world-renowned linguist Eric Lenneberg reached a similar conclusion with regard to language learning (1967):

> What is acquired are patterns and structures not constituent elements . . . We are discovering a basic process that is reflected in language as well as many other aspects of behavior. It consists of *first grasping the whole that is subsequently further differentiated* [my emphasis], each of the specifics arriving at different times and being subordinated to the whole by a process of temporal integration (pp.281-286).

We can demonstrate what Werner and Lenneberg were saying by considering how we learned to drive a car. For years, we watched drivers, some more accomplished than others. Then some loving, trusting soul agreed to help us try our hand at it. But did we *sit in the driveway* pushing the accelerator and the brakes, turning the steering wheel and changing the gears? No! A risk to other motorists and ourselves, we got out on the highway and *drove the car*, very inexpertly at first. Gradually, with more practice, we were able to concentrate our attention on the various specific skills: turning corners, stopping and starting more smoothly, even passing other cars.

If our "teacher" had demanded a perfect performance from the start and had been constantly and carpingly corrective, we would have either given up or found another teacher who would let us practice inexpertly, offering, at appropriate moments, gentle reminders about what we might concentrate on next. Eventually, by trial and error, we became reasonable drivers, although we may still think about ways to improve our performance.

Reading is best learned the same way — but Laura was expected to learn to drive her "reading machine" by sitting in the driveway, turning the wheel and operating the brakes, accelerator and transmission without being able to engage in the whole process and "put it all together." She could not relate her out-of-context learning to what she was being asked to do: read. Because she was forced to concentrate her attention on one difficult, meaningless, complex and extremely abstract aspect of the task, she could not use her natural learning strategies. Almost certainly, also, she had been expected to perform the total process in errorless ways from the beginning, thereby reducing, if not eliminating, her ability to take risks and self-correct her learning. Like the unsuccessful driver, she would probably give up trying to learn because, unlike the unsuccessful driver who had the *choice* to stop or obtain another "teacher," Laura would be made to continue with the same, or similar, teachers.

Laura Beth, on the other hand, had been given the opportunity to take control of her "reading machine" by engaging in the whole process from the start. She had been "out on the road" from the very beginning and had quickly learned to keep her car going and on track, thereby getting the feel of the whole process through repeated, and often self-directed, practice. Gradually, she was able to concentrate her attention on the component parts of the process, to become more and more adept at using them — but always in context of the whole task. Instead of having to achieve a perfect performance from the beginning, she had been encouraged to approximate and take risks. Instead of receiving constant correction, she had been provided with supportive demonstrations. In response, she had developed her own timetable, had learned to self-direct, self-correct and self-monitor her learning and to develop and integrate her own strategies in order to gain control of the process as quickly as possible.

Creating a love of books

How can we expect children to want to learn to read if they have seldom seen reading used in pleasurable ways, or if they never participate in the activity? Too often we expect them to want to learn to read because we know it is important for them to do so. In our anxiety to help them on their way, we often neglect to give them the chance to *create within themselves* a strong desire to become independent readers.

Several years ago, I had the good fortune to interview a mother of seven children who lived in Lawrencetown, Nova Scotia. She had left school in grade nine, for economic reasons, and her husband had left in grade eight. Yet all of their children were reading independently by the time they first entered school, or soon after. I asked her what she and her husband had done that helped the children learn to read so early. She replied quite simply, "We read to them."

They had been read to virtually every day from soon after their births. Each evening, this growing family would gather on the parents' bed for bedtime stories. The older children would share in reading to the younger ones. When I visited, three different books were being read aloud at these sessions, by different members.

The house was full of books. An old reel-to-reel tape recorder had also been used for many years to record and play back their frequent efforts to dramatize stories that had particular appeal. Picture-story books, fiction and factual books, Kipling, Dickens and even Shakespeare, on occasion, were part of the regular sharing of books. Many of the more popular ones were read again and again, at the request of the children. But when I asked the mother if she had ever tried to teach her children to read she exclaimed, "Teach them to read? I wouldn't know how!"

She had been an early reader herself. She distinctly remembered being puzzled when she observed her teachers trying to teach other students in her room "the sounds of the letters." She could not recall having to learn them as she learned to read. Fortunately, her teachers allowed her to continue reading independently during the reading instruction periods — although no doubt they were somewhat mystified as to how this child had managed to learn to read without the "benefits" of their teaching. She could not, in fact, remember how she had learned to read, no more than she could remember how she had learned to talk. She clearly recalled, however, that she had been read to regularly by her own mother. She still had some of her childhood books and had read them to her children. Interestingly, she never knew at what stage of their development her own children had gained their independence as readers. It was only when they actually demonstrated their ability to read new stories to her, or to other members of the family, that she realized they had mastered the task. She saw nothing unusual in the fact that all of them had learned to read so easily and so early. It had all seemed perfectly natural to her!

How and why children learn

Children are born with an immense capacity and an inner compulsion to learn. What and how they learn are very much the result of their life experiences: what they see, what they hear, what they touch, what they smell, what they participate in, and how they are encouraged to participate — all these play a crucial role in their learning. They learn what is shared with them. It is very difficult, if not impossible, to stop children from learning. It is equally difficult, if not impossible, for children to learn about something they have not shared in.

Parents smile and chatter to their babies. Before long, their babies are smiling and chattering back at them. Parents set about washing the family car. Before long, toddler sons and daughters are trying it out with the hose and the mop. Mothers and fathers sit down and read to their children. Very soon, the children are sitting with their books trying to retrieve the experience for themselves. They have begun to learn to read.

Most of what I have discovered about how children learn to read has come, and continues to come, from watching them engaged in the process of doing so. I have observed them in their homes and classrooms, and have interacted with them about their books and their writing. I have talked with their parents and their teachers about their progress. I have audiotaped, videotaped and recorded notes of my observations and experiences.

It was not until I started to observe young children actually engaged in the process of becoming readers, primarily through their own self-directed efforts, that I began to understand how reading can and should be learned as easily and naturally as talking and listening. I began to understand why it is that children who learn to read early almost invariably come from book-oriented homes, where they have been read to regularly from very early in their lives. My observations also led me to understand why far too many children find learning to read such a difficult and demanding task. When parents do not provide their preschool children with the opportunity to discover and share in the pleasures of what lies between the covers of books, they are making learning to read a much more difficult task than it ought to be, just as they would make learning to talk very difficult if they did not talk to their children. Similarly, when teachers place an emphasis on the skills of reading *before* children have obtained a wide and rewarding experience with books and reading, they set up barriers to their progress towards becoming proficient readers.

Reading begins at birth

Reading to a child on the day of its birth may seem to verge on the ridiculous. But "a picture is worth a thousand words" — the photographs on the following pages provide some justification for the claim. When I show an audience the first picture, of our son Raja being read to by his mother at the grand age of 6 hours, invariably a ripple of derisive laughter runs through the group. Why would we read to a child so young? What would the child gain from such an experience? I also comment that Diana read occasionally to Raja during the last two months of her pregnancy — disbelief is often the reaction.

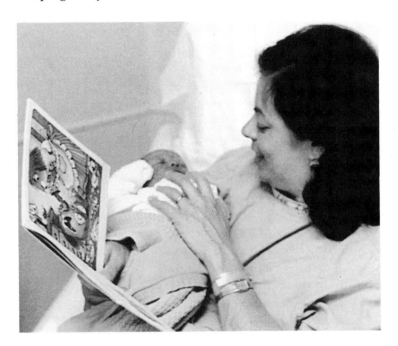

Laughter and feelings of doubt quickly disappear, however, and thoughtful silence takes their place when I show them the next picture, of Raja being read to at 2 months. I then ask the question, "Could he have developed such an obvious interest in books if he had not been read to during the first two months of his life?" The audience's understanding and interest grow as we begin to discuss what young children can learn from being read to from birth.

We did not start reading to Raja on the day he was born to make him into an early reader. We knew, of course, that by reading to him regularly we would be contributing to his reading development, but we knew also that he would make use of the experience in whatever way he saw fit. We both love reading, and especially enjoy reading to children. We are convinced that all children who grow up in a society that places a high value on its members becoming fully literate *have the right to be read to from as early in their lives as possible.* Any delay in providing them with this experience may be just as harmful to their written language development as failing to talk to them from the time they are born is harmful to their oral language development. If we want our children to take control of the process of learning to read and write for themselves, then it is important that we immerse them in books and the language of books soon after they are born.

For the first few months of their lives, children are a captive audience. They cannot escape from what we choose to do to and with them. We talk to them. We sing to them. So why not give them the opportunity to hear the crafted, memorable and lilting language of books? Why not begin to let them form positive associations with books through being held securely and lovingly in their parents' arms as they are read and reread stories, poems, nursery rhymes and jingles? Why not give them the opportunity to learn to let their imaginations work for them through what they are hearing and seeing? Why not give them the chance to experience all kinds of emotions vicariously as they learn to deal with fear and courage, good and evil, love and hate, and so on? The warm human sharing that occurs when parents, children and their books come together lays an essential foundation for the further development of the children as readers. Books and reading are given the chance to become associated permanently with these experiences and feelings in totally natural circumstances.

By the time Raja was 2 months old, it was clear that he had already begun to establish an interest in being read to. He was in his rocker one day and began to cry. I picked up a book that had been read and reread to him (Mercer Mayer's *Just For You*), held it in front of him and began to read it. His cries were stilled immediately and his eyes focused on the pages and never moved from them. I read two more familiar stories with the same result. We found that familiar books, even by this stage of his development, were superb pacifiers. His loudest cries could be stilled by simply starting to read one to him.

By 4 months, Raja's interest in books had already reached the avid stage. By this time he could distinguish between stories that had been read and reread to him and those that were new. Perhaps most surprisingly, he could do this with books read in either English or Arabic! One day Diana was reading a familiar story to him in English while I watched, trying to gauge his degree of attentiveness. He was obviously extremely interested, sitting very still, looking

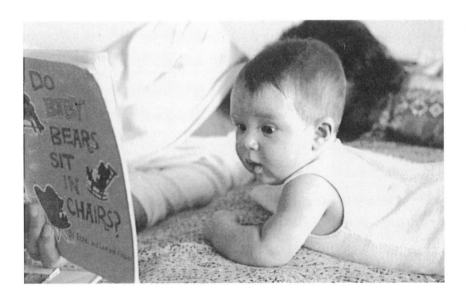

carefully at each page as it was read. His mother then picked up an unfamiliar book. By the time she had read two or three pages, he had begun to grow restless and reached out to push the book away. At my prompting, the same procedure was repeated twice, with the same result. Each time the familiar story was read, his attentiveness returned, and each time a new one was started, an almost immediate loss of interest occurred. When the familiar and unfamiliar books were written in Arabic, the same avid attention was given to the familiar one and a growing disinterest displayed in the unfamiliar one.

We found it did not take long for a book to become familiar to Raja, however. One or two readings and he was "hooked." It was a simple matter to read new books to him as he was lying in his crib or rocker, or as he was being fed. Some books were accepted on their first reading, particularly highly predictable ones with rhyming, repetitive and cumulative patterns in their language. John Langstaff's *Over in the Meadow* demonstrated this. Raja began to chuckle at the repetitive lines:

> "Dig," said the Mother.
> "I dig," said the one.
> So he dug and was glad in the sand in the sun.

His chuckle grew to laughter, which became more hilarious as the lines continued to be repeated throughout the story. The story is still a firm favorite with him.

Some parents and teachers tend to stop reading to children who demonstrate a loss of interest in what is being read. While it is counter-productive to attempt to force the children to continue listening, it may well be that they simply need time to become familiar with the language of the story through repeated readings. Presenting it to them a few pages at a time, but always commencing the reading at the beginning of the story, provides an opportunity for them to build this familiarity.

Predictable books, such as Sarah Barchas's *I Was Walking Down the Road*, or Walter Einsel's *Did You Ever See?*, for example, have a particularly important role to play in children's early reading development. Children very quickly become familiar with their language. They can begin to anticipate certain repeated sequences, even during the first reading of the book. The repeated rhythmic and rhyming nature of the language provides them with another avenue for the rapid acquisition of a new story into their repertoire of favorites. It would seem that even before young children have control over their ability to produce recognizable oral language, they can learn to "read along" with the reader and enjoy the process of sharing a familiar story.

There is probably no more emotionally secure experience for a child than to be held in the arms of a loving parent and read to on a regular basis. The warmth of feeling, the sense of belonging, and the melodic and reassuringly familiar sound of the parent's voice flowing almost directly into the child's ear provide a situation that is sought again and again. Very soon, this intense and pervasive feeling of pleasure becomes associated with books and reading, and books themselves come to be viewed as sources of this pleasure. The foundations are being laid for the children to want to learn to read, to want to make books their own, in order to be able to gain access to the activity they already know can gave them so much enjoyment and security.

A sense of this enjoyment and security is reflected in Raja's expression in the following photograph, taken as Diana was reading to him at the age of 6 months.

By this time, his attention seemed to last as long as we were prepared to read to him. As we read certain parts of some stories, he would respond with excited wriggles, stretching and arm-waving. This was particularly noticeable when we read some featured print such as *MEOW!*, *BOOM!* or *NO----OOOO!* with appropriate emphasis. It was clear that he was already beginning to predict what was coming next in a familiar story — his change in behavior indicated that he was actually anticipating some words *before* they were read to him. Even by this early stage of his development, he was learning intuitively to engage in the predicting-confirming process so vital to fluent reading.

It did not take Raja long to understand that his books had to be treated with care. For a time, we would leave one of his familiar books propped up in his crib, opened at a page with a particularly detailed and colorful illustration. We found that he would lie and inspect the illustration very carefully for long periods of time and eventually drop off to sleep. One day, however, we found that he had managed to reach out and grasp the book, had somehow been able to tear out the page with the illustration on it, and had proceeded to crumple it up and find out what it tasted like. For a time after that, we left only books with cardboard pages when he was unattended.

Over the next few months, we took care to demonstrate how to turn pages carefully and how to hold a book with two hands, talking to Raja all the time about what we were doing and why we were doing it. Gradually, we gave him more and more opportunity to handle books with regular paper pages, quietly admonishing him when he was in danger of tearing a page and providing him with another demonstration of what he should be doing. By 9 to 10 months, it was clear he had learned his books had to be handled with care. It was around

this time that we began to notice him sitting for periods of up to 45 minutes holding a book and carefully turning its pages, obviously intent on mastering the technique required to do this independently. It was evident also that he knew the pages of English books were to be turned in one direction and Arabic ones in the opposite!

Perhaps one of the most significant aspects of Raja's early reading development went vitually unnoticed until we looked at a videotape of his independent play with books. Although the two preceding photographs show how he was learning to manipulate a book physically, they cannot indicate the sounds he often made as he engaged in this type of activity. As we looked at the videotape, we realized that as early as 6 months he was not only beginning to act like a reader as he lay and held a book and tried to turn its pages, but he was making unintelligible sounds each time he managed to turn a page. By 10 months, these sounds were even more "reading-like," as he sat and skillfully turned the pages of the book he was "reading." Since he would sit for long periods of time engaged in this type of behavior, one can assume that he was already retrieving his favorite stories for himself in the only way he knew how: by acting like a reader. Although we will never have any way of knowing, it may well be that he was actually obtaining varying degrees of meaning for himself from this activity, despite the fact that at this stage of his development he could not produce recognizable language.

I have offered this rather detailed description of Raja's early learning development to demonstrate how children can be "hooked on books" from a very early age. During the first year of his life, he was read to for an average of approximately one hour a day. There were very few days when he was not read to. On some, we would share books for two hours and more. He also had a cassette recorder in his room and tapes of music, stories and nursery rhymes which were played to him as he relaxed in his crib or play area. Rarely did he miss his bedtime stories. Both of us read to him, with Diana spending about twice as much time as I did. It was a simple, enjoyable and immensely rewarding experience to share his ever-growing library of books with him on a regular basis and to realize how much this sharing meant to him.

Conclusion

The sooner we start reading to children, the easier it is for reading to become an integral part of their daily lives. The later we start, the harder this becomes. Children are born with an enormous imaginative potential, but unless that wellspring is tapped and given opportunity to develop, it will lie idle and unstimulated, eventually atrophying through lack of use. It may be, even, that children have a "developmental need" to have their imaginations stimulated. Where the home does not provide this kind of experience for children, the school has an immensely important role to play. It has to make up for the loss of five or six years of optimum learning time. Sharing books with children on their entry to school must then form an essential part of their daily experience.

Developing a love of books and an inner drive to learn to read is only the first step in children's progress towards gaining access to the printed word in all its forms — but a vitally important one. It leads to further opportunities for them to self-direct their learning. Once they learn that books provide pleasures that can be obtained in no other way, they are on their way to becoming readers in the real sense of the word.

Learning the language of books

**"And Joseph couldn't get them a room 'cause
all the motels were overbooked."**

The Bil Keane cartoon above illustrates what this chapter is all about. The "reader" is reproducing her own version of one of her favorite stories "on the run," using some of the language of the book and some of her own. Despite her alterations to the language used by the author, she maintains the meaning of the original story. If we could hear her, she would be "reading" confidently and expressively. In fact, she is acting like a reader in nearly every respect.

Reading-like behavior

Most parents who have read to their preschool children on a regular basis have had the experience of omitting part of a favorite story, either by accident or by design, only to be told immediately and very firmly that they have missed something and need to reread correctly. On other occasions, they were surprised to discover that their children could somehow reproduce the whole of a favorite story for themselves, perhaps not accurately at the word level, but with a high degree of similarity at the meaning level, turning the pages of the book at precisely the appropriate points in the story.

How do children learn to retrieve stories in this manner? Why do they do it? How is written language different from spoken language? What role does gaining control over book language have in the process of learning to read? These are some of the questions this chapter will answer.

How do children learn book language?

Gillian had been read to virtually from birth. I asked her father when he thought his daughter had started learning to reproduce her stories in reading-like ways:

> It's hard to tell. How do you know when a child tries to memorize? She'd listen. Then all of a sudden, she would repeat the whole thing, or large passages of it. She always paid careful attention when you read it. I guess she was absorbing the story.

"Absorbing the story." An interesting and, as we will see, appropriate observation!

Are children like blotting paper for the language and meaning of their stories? The analogy seems to provide a useful description of the process. However, unlike the way blotting paper soaks up ink, rendering it unusable, children seem able to preserve the language they absorb and use it again to reconstruct the meaning of their stories with increasing competence.

I also asked Gillian's father how he thought she could learn to reproduce so many stories in reading-like ways, sometimes after only a few shared readings. He replied thoughtfully and again insightfully:

> I don't think she really tries to memorize the stories. It's more of an osmosis.

A vision of this little girl sharing a favorite book with her father comes to my mind. As she listens, the meaning and words of the story flow into her ears and filter through to the language centers of her brain, to become part of her existing network of thoughts and feelings. At the same time, her imagination and emotions are being provided with suitable nutrients to add breadth and depth to the thoughts and feelings. More colors and patterns are added to an existing, already rich and constantly shifting mosaic — like a dye that, when added to a liquid, effortlessly permeates it, changing its color, sometimes a little, sometimes quite markedly. The language of Gillian's stories permeates her brain, constantly embellishing, amending and enlarging her existing verbal "data bank" without conscious effort on her part. The concept of osmosis may be an entirely appropriate way to describe the processes involved.

The remarkable ability of young children to absorb the meaning and language of their stories and to reproduce these in reading-like ways has been described by Marie Clay (1979) and Don Holdaway (1979). Clay first referred to it as children "talking like a book." Holdaway saw it as a process of "re-enactment," although he also uses the term "reading-like behavior." I use the latter term in this book. However, I make a distinction between "fluent" reading-like behavior, where children retrieve their stories with little or no attention to the print on the pages, and "arhythmic" reading-like behavior, where they begin to slow the process down and commence to match what they are saying with what they are seeing on the printed pages of their books.

Although they are the best we have at the moment, in a sense those terms diminish our understanding of the process. To children, there is nothing "reading-like" in their story reading. Until they begin to realize that the *print* on the page plays an important role in reading, they legitimately view themselves as readers. Gillian was 5 years 7 months (5.7) when I asked her if she could read, with her eyes closed, a page of the book we had been sharing. She immediately did, with great confidence, perfect expression and absolute accuracy:

> The wind blows on the window pane,
> The rain falls on the ground,
> I think I'll go and have some tea,
> And read this book I've found.

When I asked her if she was really reading, she pointed out with righteous indignation in her voice, "That's what it says!" And she was right, of course!

The contribution of reading-like behavior to the process of learning to read has been vastly underestimated in the past. The reasons for this were expressed, almost inadvertently, by the mother of two children I had been observing, when I asked her what she thought of their ability to retrieve so many of their stories through the use of reading-like behavior:

> Oh, I thought it was cute! In fact, it amazed me how many stories they could memorize.

To classify such complex behavior as "cute" clearly devalues its true significance. To view it as a product of rote memorization based on repetitive patterning is to misunderstand the sophisticated nature of the processes.

As I looked at many transcripts of children actively involved in reproducing their stories, it became obvious that reading-like behavior is the result of a drive on the part of the children to gain control over their books for themselves. Children intuitively use a variety of self-generated strategies. Rather than being "cute," their behavior is purposeful, sophisticated and sustained, and directed quite specifically at providing them with independent access to their favorite books.

It also became quite clear that, rather than relying on rote memorization of the words of their stories, children absorb the central meanings of those stories and, as a result, use language in highly creative ways. They combine their own language with that of the author, frequently engaging in skillful transformations to maintain the flow of the story. Sometimes they even improve the quality of the language used in the original version!

Unfortunately, transcripts cannot communicate what I also heard: the children's "readings" were intonationally alive. Through the use of their voices, they identified character, atmosphere, action and climax. In short, their behavior revealed that what they were doing was a far cry from mindless regurgitation. Rather, they exhibited the result of their intrinsic desire to represent what their stories meant to them *at the deepest possible level.*

Reading-like behavior has to be accepted for what it is: a developmentally based, intrinsically motivated language-learning strategy used by young children to control, for themselves, the process of gaining independent access to an activity that has given them countless hours of pleasure in the company of others. Just as they maintain control over their own oral language development, so, too, do they want to gain control over their written language learning.

They do not have to be *made* to listen to certain stories again and again. They *demand* that this happen with a range of selected favorites. They do not have to be *made* to reproduce these stories in reading-like ways. Provided someone reads to them, *inviting but never demanding* their participation in the reading, participate they will. They do not have to be *made* to focus their attention on the meaningful reconstruction of their stories. They do so because it would not make sense to do it any other way. Young children are gifted language learners, and learning to read is a language-learning task. If we supply them with the necessary conditions and experiences, they will continue to find effective ways of self-directing their learning-to-read processes.

Why learn the language of books?

Languages differ in their spoken and written forms. In some, both the structure (syntax) and the words of the written form are quite different from those used in the spoken form — in Arabic, for example. Languages that possess this characteristic are called diglossic. Being able to speak the colloquial form of a diglossic language provides very little basis for being able to learn to read its written form.

In English, these differences are not so apparent. The greater similarity between its spoken and written forms has almost certainly contributed to the widely accepted view that, as long as they can speak, children are "ready" to learn to read and write. The assumption is that the spoken language form is *primary*, while the written form is derived, or *secondary*. In other words, learning the written form of the language is dependent upon a certain level of competence in the use of the spoken form.

Although this is not often acknowledged, these assumptions have had some disastrous effects on the way reading has been taught and tested in our schools. Since reading has been seen as the process of learning to recognize words that are already known and used in spoken language, the main aim of instruction has been to teach children to recognize those words. Since words are made up of letters which, in various combinations or alone, represent the variety of sounds used in spoken language, the initial focus of instruction has been on teaching the range of letter-sound relationships (phonics) and all the rules that are supposed to govern them. If they master these, the children will be able to use their knowledge to recognize any words they already know (and perhaps some they do not) and to read independently.

It all sounds very simple and logical. Unfortunately this view is based on an entirely false premise. We do *not* learn language that way! We do not start with meaningless bits and pieces (letters, sounds and words in isolation). We start with whole, meaningful language. We speak to our children from the time of their birth in whole sentences. We read whole stories to them. We provide them with the opportunity to learn to talk and read by using whatever they can from these experiences with language to make sense of and interact with the world around them. From birth, the emphasis is on functional, meaningful language and on giving children control of the learning process for themselves. We have a plethora of evidence demonstrating that these are the basic conditions needed for children to learn *to speak and listen*. We now have an extensive and ever-growing body of evidence telling us, with a great deal of certainty, that these are the same basic conditions needed for them to learn to read and write.

Learning to read, then, should *not* be seen as dependent on some predetermined level of competence in spoken language. Learning the written and spoken language systems should be seen as interdependent and mutually supportive. In order to learn to read as fluently and easily as they learn to talk, *children have to establish control over the oral dimensions of written language.* In other words, they have to become as familiar as possible with the language of the books they are reading.

How are spoken and written language different?

I frequently attend conferences where professors deliver to teachers learned papers on the research they have been conducting. They read what they have written for publication in some scholarly journal. I am not surprised that many "lose" their audience very quickly. Blank expressions appear on the faces of those present, and some of the more courageous simply get up from their seats and leave. To expect an audience to be able to listen to and understand complex expository prose that is being read to them is expecting the impossible. Our memory systems simply cannot handle all the information coming in at a steady pace determined by the reader, and in the more complex form of written language.

The most obvious distinction between spoken and written language is that spoken language usually occurs in conversational settings. It is "situationally bound." Most of its meaning is related to and supported by the situation in which it occurs, and is assisted by intonation, gesture, facial expression and other "body language." Spoken language is often incomplete and uncrafted, usually composed of short, uncomplicated sentences. Redundancies and repetitions are frequent. Ambiguities are tolerated because the situation provides immediate, meaningful support. "Over there . . . " cannot mean "over their . . . " Anophoric references such as *these, those, this* and *that* can be identified simply by looking. When the listener does not comprehend, the speaker provides clarification, often through elaboration. The "here and now" nature of spoken language, therefore, does not often place demands on the listener for complex mental images to make sense of what is being said.

Most written language, on the other hand, is not situationally bound. While print in such places as the supermarket, on road signs or on television advertisements has an "environment," we know that when we are reading a story, a poem, a magazine or a newspaper it is the print alone that carries the message. Instead of being able to refer to the speaker for clarification of meaning, readers are thrown almost completely on their own resources. Written language is required to carry the total load of meaning, without any ambiguity. Therefore, it is much more formal and complex, more highly crafted and polished, and it possesses few redundancies. Pronouns are used freely, often at a considerable distance from their reference points. Various literary genres — narrative and expository prose, poetry and plays — are distinct from each other in their structure and format. Even within each genre there are many different styles. The "removed and distant" nature of written language places considerable demands on the reader's own mental images to create meaning in the absence of direct, sensory support.

It is not difficult to see the implications for learning to read. Without some knowledge of written language forms, gained from countless hours of book-sharing experiences, reconstructing meaning from the non-situational language of books becomes a difficult and often impossible task for children, whether listening to a story or trying to read one for themselves. Illustrations can help, but they are no real substitute for the kind of directly visual and active support children are accustomed to using in interpreting spoken language. Meaning from books has to be reconstructed from the reader's or listener's own inner resources.

One such resource is the ability to make predictions when listening to or reading text, in order to maintain the flow of meaning. If I stop typing in the middle of a _____, you will probably be _____ to fill in the missing _____. If I provide you with the first l_____ of each w_____, you will be able to f_____ in the g_____ with even greater e_____. You can do that because you are reasonably familiar with the patterns of written language, and you want to make some sense of what I am writing. Although you may not have inserted the exact words I would have used (*sentence, able, words, letter, word, fill, gaps, ease*), I am sure the ones you used made sense and sounded like language.

As efficient speakers and listeners, readers and writers, we constantly engage in prediction. Provided we are familiar with the patterns and structures of written language, we are able to predict with a fair degree of success what is coming next on the page, *before* we see the actual word or words. We confirm our predictions on the basis of information constantly available to us. We have a need to make sense of what we read in terms of what we already know. We want to make what we are reading sound like the language we know. As the final stage in the confirming process, we select as little or as much visual information (the print on the page) as we need to. When our predictions are not confirmed, we go back and take another run at what we are reading. The greater our familiarity with the language of books and the topic about which we are reading, the less we need to use the print itself.

Asking young children to read an unfamiliar book without first having gained control over its language structures is like asking them to learn to ride a bicycle with square wheels. To do so, the rider would have to concentrate constantly on balancing the machine rather than on keeping it going and letting the matter of balance take care of itself. Under these conditions, riding would never become a flowing, enjoyable and emotionally rewarding experience. Similarly, reading that is fluent, enjoyable and emotionally rewarding can be achieved only when readers do *not* have to focus their attention on the letters and words, but can use their knowledge of book language to continuously predict what is coming next on the page.

Fluent reading-like behavior

I asked Gillian (5.4) how she had learned to "read" the story she had just shared with me. She explained quite blithely: "Well, they keep reading it to me and I keep following it." When I asked her how she had managed to learn so many of her stories in this manner, she replied simply, "Well, I just do it!" It was all very natural and normal to her. She could reproduce most of the 150 books in her personal library with varying degrees of accuracy, using fluent reading-like behavior. Learning to read was a very simple process for Gillian at this point, although later, as she became aware of the role of print, she was to view it in a rather different light (see pages 51-54).

The importance of storytime

By its very nature, storytime is a shared experience that invites participation on the part of children. Given the opportunity to listen to favorite stories read repeatedly, young children will usually demonstrate a strong desire to join in the reading in a variety of ways. They may *mumble read* along with the reader, occasionally finishing off a line as the reader pauses at some predictable point in the story. *Completion reading* becomes more pronounced as the story continues to be reread, with the reader sometimes having to provide only the first word of a sentence or line as a cue. Children will also *echo read* a line or phrase or sentence that has just been read to them. And as their confidence and familiarity with the story grows, they may engage in *cooperative reading*, where they endeavor to read along with the reader, taking the lead at times, and at times reading in unison or trailing just behind the reader's voice with their own. These strategies are developed and used intuitively by children in their efforts to gain independent access to stories. Which they use is influenced by the manner in which the stories are read to them, the nature of the language in the stories, the type of support and encouragement they receive from the reader to participate and, sometimes, the strength of their desire to make the stories their own.

The following two transcripts are from recordings of parents reading to their children. Both demonstrate very clearly that the way parents or teachers support and encourage them plays an important role in children's willingness to participate in reading-like ways.

Kaaren (4.5) and Sean (3.1) were being read to by their mother. Jan Pienkowski's *Meg on the Moon* had been read to them several times already and was becoming a favorite. The story starts with a "countdown" and the mother (M) tried to have Kaaren (K) and Sean (S) participate in the reading:

M: I'll start at the countdown. Here comes the countdown! Ten! Maybe you
    could count with me. Nine! (Pauses, inviting the children to participate.)

K/S: Nine (with some uncertainty in their voices).

M: Eight!

K: Eight. (Sean does not attempt a response.)

M: What's this (pointing to the 7)?

K/S: (Both mumble an unintelligible response.)

M: (Points to the 6.)

S: Eight.

K: Nine.

M: No! Six. Nine's up there (pointing to the 9). What's that (pointing to the 5)?

K: Five (again with some hesitation in her voice).

M: (Points to the 4.) Joe (her nickname for Sean)?

S: Seven (very uncertainly).

M: No!

S: (Immediately) I don't want to talk right now (stated loudly and emphatically)!

What was Sean saying to his mother? "I don't want to play this game anymore!" "I don't want to take any more risks!" "Just leave me out of this activity." Sean knew he was supposed to say something, in this case a number, so he said the one he could remember. In the language sense, his response was entirely acceptable. As his mother (uneccesarily) corrected him, however, he quickly found that his answer was not acceptable, and he decided to avoid the possibility of making another mistake in front of his mother and his sister.

Contrast Sean's experience with that of Adrienne (1.6!), who was being invited to share in the third reading of Bill Martin's *Brown Bear, Brown Bear*. She had been read to virtually from birth. Adrienne's contribution to the reading has been underlined; the vertical brackets enclosing two lines indicate when the words were said almost simultaneously:

Text	Adrienne and her mother
I see a blue horse	I see a (mother pauses) . . . blue
Looking at me.	(pauses again) . . . <u>house</u>
	⎡ looking (pauses)
	⎣ <u>look</u> . . . <u>at</u> <u>me</u>.
	<u>Tail!</u> (Adrienne points to the tail on the horse.) Yes. (Mother responds and continues reading.)
Blue horse	Blue horse
Blue horse	<u>Blue</u> <u>horse</u>
What do you see?	What do you see? (pauses) . . . <u>see?</u>
I see a gray mouse	I see a (pauses) . . . <u>gay</u> <u>mouse</u>
Looking at me.	Looking (pauses) . . . at me.
Gray mouse	Gray mouse
Gray mouse	⎡ <u>Gay</u> <u>mouse</u>
What do you see?	⎣ <u>Gay</u> <u>mouse</u>
	What do you see?
I see a green frog	I see a (pauses) . . . <u>yellow</u> <u>fwog</u>
Looking at me.	Looking (pauses) . . . at me.
Green frog	⎡ Green frog
Green frog	⎣ <u>fwog</u>
	⎡ Green frog
	⎣ <u>Gween</u>

The whole book was read in this shared manner, with Adrienne constantly participating enthusiastically and confidently. Her mother never directly corrected any "miscues," but simply continued reading, modeling the process and pausing at points where she intuitively felt that her daughter could complete the line. Adrienne almost invariably corrected her own miscues, as she did with *house/horse* and *yellow/green*. *Gay/gray* was not corrected simply because the gr sound was impossible for her to make at this stage of her language development.

Experimentation and approximation

When children learn to talk, their efforts to produce oral language in some form is almost always met with approval, attention and pleasure on the part of their parents, no matter how unrecognizable the sounds may be. All over the world, parents seem to accept instinctively the principles of experimentation and approximation, and couple it with an immediate and positive response to any attempts made by their children to produce oral language. Children are constantly encouraged to play with language-making in purposeful ways, and their productive efforts are rarely subjected to correction. Adults know intuitively that their role is simply to model language being used appropriately, to invite children to participate in experimental ways in producing meaningful communication, and to respond to their efforts in supportive and non-corrective ways. They trust their children as learners of oral language.

9-11

"We don't say 'I losed my dime.' We say 'I LOSTED it.' "

But with written language learning, unfortunately, the pattern is quite different. The expectation is that children should be able to read and write accurately from their first attempts. No warm and affectionate response greets the production of reading and writing that only vaguely resembles the accurate adult model. Too many adults judge children's first attempts by standards of adult accuracy. Their approximating efforts are usually met with an immediate corrective and often negatively oriented reaction on the part of parents and teachers, which quickly informs them of their failure. This response denies children the opportunity to engage in the self-correction that helps to develop their own delicate feedback mechanisms. There is no surer and quicker way to stop children from learning (and from *wanting* to learn) than for adults to engage in a constant process of correction based on their conception of what is and is not acceptable.

In both oral and written language, children learn most effectively when they are encouraged to try things out for themselves, take risks and make mistakes, and when they learn to self-correct as a result of monitoring their own behavior. Adrienne was given the opportunity to learn to reproduce her books in non-corrective and supportive ways, and she responded by continuing to involve herself actively in the process of learning their language. Sean, on the other hand, experienced immediate and negative feedback for his effort to participate in the reading and, predictably, wanted no part of the situation.

Focus on meaning

4-19

"Then the caterpillar puts on his butterfly costume and flies away."

As children attempt to retrieve their favorite stories for themselves in reading-like ways, they invariably focus their efforts on reproducing meaning.

They are seldom concerned with achieving a surface accuracy at the word level. The following transcripts reveal how they go about doing this.

The first was recorded when Sean (2.11) and Kaaren (4.3) were sharing the reading of Eric Carle's *The Very Hungry Caterpillar* with their mother. Throughout the reading, she paused and prompted their joint and individual participation in healthy ways. Since Kaaren knew the story better than Sean and was, of course, far more advanced in her language development, she tended to dominate the participation. She had just completed reproducing an extended section of the story with tremendous fluency and had run out of breath. Sean was determined to have his say, saw his chance and came in with great gusto. The parts of the original text that were transformed by him have been underlined:

Text	Sean
The day was Sunday again. The caterpillar ate through one nice green leaf and then he felt much better.	But Tuesday (self-corrects) . . . on Tuesday, he ate through one green leaf and then he feeled much better.

Since every day of the week was Tuesday for Sean, it was not surprising that day was substituted for Sunday. His self-correction of "But Tuesday" to "On Tuesday" could have been made because of the repetitive pattern already used by the author, or because Sean realized that it would not "fit" with what he was going to say next. It was probably the result of a combination of these two factors. But most impressive was the skillful manner in which this very young boy collapsed the two sentences into one, maintaining both the meaning and the tense of the original. He transformed *the caterpillar* into the pronoun "he" and constructed his own past tense form of the verb *to feel* by simply adding the past tense marker *ed* to it. He almost certainly had not learned the irregular form *felt* yet, and "feeled" sounded right to his ear. Reconstructing meaning or rote memorization? Sean answers this question for us very clearly!

Jennifer grew up in a book-oriented home and had been read to almost from birth. She owned an extensive library of books and would often wake up through the night and take one of them to her parents to read to her. She would also sometimes be found asleep over her books, with her light on, even though she had been read numerous bedtime stories before her light had been turned off for the night!

The following transcript was recorded when she was 3.10. She was deeply immersed in "reading" Paul Galdone's version of *The Three Bears*. Her reconstruction was fluent, supremely confident and intonationally alive. The parts of the text she altered have been underlined for the purpose of clarity:

Text	Jennifer
The three bears went into the bedroom.	And they went into their bedroom.
"Somebody has been lying in my bed!" said the Great Big Bear in his great big voice.	And the Daddy said, "Somebody was sleeping in my bed!" (Read in a very deep voice.)
"Somebody has been lying in my bed!" said the Middle-Sized Bear in her middle-sized voice.	And the Mummy said, "Somebody was sleeping in my bed!" (Read in a "middle-sized" voice.)
"Somebody has been lying in my bed and here she is!" cried the Little Wee Bear in his little wee voice.	And the baby one said, "Somebody was sleeping in my bed and here she is!" (Read in a very small voice.)

Not only was Jennifer able to recompose the way direct speech was used in the story, she also substituted "they" for *the three bears*, "Daddy" for *the Great Big Bear*, "Mummy" for *the Middle-Sized Bear* and "Baby" for *the Little Wee Bear*. The past tense form *had been lying* was replaced with the past tense form "was sleeping" — and she was able to make all these transformations without losing any meaning! All of this was done "on the run" and with an obvious feeling of enjoyment and of personal satisfaction. She used her voice in quite a dramatic manner to represent the three story characters.

Gillian was a master at reconstructing versions of her favorite stories. I asked her father whether he thought she deliberately set out to memorize the words of her stories:

> She *knows* [his emphasis] the story. She knows the *content* [his emphasis] of the story — almost any story! Sometimes when a new book comes, for example, and [her mother] has read it to her and she shows it to me the first time, she tells me the story.

The following transcript provides us with an excellent example of how skillful this girl (just 5.7) had become at "knowing the content" of her stories. She had received the book *Bambi, Thumper and Me* from the Disney Book Club approximately one month before this recording was made. Despite the fact that it was 39 pages long, with a considerable amount of text on each page, she had managed to gain control over the content of the story and was able to retrieve most of it in the manner represented in the transcript. She read with great fluency and faultless expression. Again, I have underlined the parts of the text that have been recomposed:

Text	Gillian
"My tail!" exclaimed Thumper. <u>"What's wrong with my tail?"</u> A look of surprise came over the little rabbit's face <u>when he turned around and found it was gone.</u>	"My tail!" exclaimed Thumper. <u>"Why don't you like it?"</u> A look of surprise came over the little rabbit's face. <u>"My tail!" he said.</u> <u>"It's gone!"</u>
<u>Then while</u> they were trying to figure out what had happened,	<u>When</u> they were trying to figure out what had happened <u>over Thumper's tail,</u>
Bambi's spots began to float <u>from</u> his back <u>and fly through the air.</u>	Bambi's spots began to float <u>off</u> his back <u>into the forest.</u>
"My spots!" cried Bambi. "They're <u>flying away!"</u> And they all began <u>running</u> after the spots.	"My spots!" cried Bambi. They're <u>floating</u> away!" And they all began <u>to run</u> after the spots.

There can be little doubt that surface-level rote memorization was playing little part in Gillian's reproduction of the story. Her transformation of *What's wrong with my tail?* to "Why don't you like it?" was produced as a result of deep-level processing occurring in the language center of her brain. Her alteration to the dramatic cry "'My tail!' he said. 'It's gone!'" in place of the author's rather pedantic *when he turned around and discovered it was gone* could be seen as providing the description of this alarming turn of events in Thumper's life with considerably more impact. All of the changes she made were perfectly acceptable at the meaning and language levels — it was interesting to see how she specified where Bambi's spots were going ("into the forest") in advance of the author's reference to it.

Gillian's display of mature reading-like behavior contains all the elements of fluent adult reading except, of course, that she does not make much use of the print on the pages. She actively and intuitively predicts — there is no other way she could have maintained her smooth, controlled and uninterrupted flow of acceptable language. Her apt use of appropriate phrasing and relevant intonation patterns indicate how meaningful the content of the story had become for her. With her repertoire of productive language skills and her commitment to meaning, Gillian had the crucially important *functional* aspects of written language under control. All she had left to do was learn how to use the *form*, the visual detail of print, the third of the cueing systems independent readers employ. She had already made considerable progress in this direction, as we shall see in the next chapter when we examine the role of *arhythmic* reading-like behavior.

Growing accuracy

Provided children are read to on a regular basis from very early in their lives, and provided their "read it again" requests are met, they are capable of *absorbing* almost any kind of book language. The degree of accuracy they achieve at the word level in their attempts at *reproducing* what they hear depends on a number of factors: age, previous experience with the volume and type of language in the books being read to them, the manner in which they are invited to participate in the reading, and the desire they have to master a particular book for themselves. I believe you could read a stock market report or Shakespeare to children on a regular basis and they would eventually be able to read along with you with a surprising degree of accuracy!

If the language of the book is of the highly predictable kind found in nursery rhymes, poetry and books such as Bill Martin's *Brown Bear, Brown Bear* or Eve Sutton's *My Cat Likes to Hide in Boxes*, its accurate acquisition is relatively simple and rapid. Like the chants, songs and folktales of people whose cultures survive through the oral tradition, the rhythmic, rhyming, repetitive and often cyclically cumulative nature of the language demands active participation and absorption.

When Raja was not quite 3 years old, we had the good fortune to stay with Dorothy Butler at her beautiful beachside home in Keri Keri, New Zealand. When she presented him with a copy of her delightful collection of children's poems *For Me, Me, Me,* he wanted them to be read to him repeatedly. At the end of approximately three weeks, after literally dozens of readings, at his request, he knew virtually every poem in the book and could reproduce them very accurately and with supreme confidence. One of the first ones he learned was Eleanor Farjeon's "Cats", with its compellingly rhythmic nature:

Cats sleep anywhere,
Any table,
Any chair,
Top of piano,
Window-ledge,
In the middle,
On the edge . . .

Another one that attracted him particularly was James Kirrup's "Baby's Drinking Song," which he delighted in rattling off at great speed. Try it for yourself and feel how it rolls off the tongue!

Sip a little
Sup a little

From your little
Cup a little
Sup a little
Sip a little
Put it to your
Lip a little . . .

But we also read him poetry that was much more complex, from Satomi Ichikawa's *Under the Cherry Tree*, for instance. Poems by such people as T.S. Eliot and John Drinkwater seemed to appeal to him and it was not long before he had even these under control.

A predictable book also poses few problems for children. When we read Robert Kraus's *Whose Mouse Are You?* with its repetitive and rhyming structure, Raja was soon completing the lines as we paused in our reading, and before long was reproducing the whole story with absolute accuracy:

Whose mouse are you?
Nobody's mouse.
Where is your mother?
Inside the cat.
Where is your father?
Caught in a trap . . .

Books containing nursery rhymes, poetry and stories that use the predictable format serve a very useful purpose in promoting the reading development of young children. Because the language of these books is acquired so easily, the children quickly gain independent access to them. They have a feeling of success as language learners, and receive a tremendous boost to their confidence. From their point of view, they can "read" just like Mom and Dad. For example, when I asked Gillian whether learning to read would be easy or hard for her, she replied enthusiastically, "Easy! So easy!" Although this attitude tends to change as the children become increasingly aware of the need to learn to use print in order to read independently, behaving *like* a reader serves an extremely important purpose in *becoming* a reader.

I want to stress that it is also important to read books that contain more complex and intricate language and more well-developed and varied story structures (story grammars). Some authorities recommend reading only simple books to young children. If we want our children to learn only simple language structures, then of course we may read only simple books to them. But if we want them to understand and be able to reproduce complex and intricate book language, then we must read books with that kind of language. One of Raja's many favorite books is Tomie dePaola's *The Three Wise Kings*. Here is a transcript of his "reading" of this story at 2.8 years. He reproduced these two pages with absolute accuracy and complete confidence, having read the first page with me in a cooperative manner:

> These wise men studied the stars.
> Each night
> they looked at the sky
> and wrote down where the stars were,
> where they had come from,
> and where they were going.
> One night
> a star they had never seen before
> appeared in the sky.
> Each of the kings consulted his books
> and found that this new star was the sign
> that a great king was about to be born.

At this point he commented on the illustration: "Look at this huge church!"

The sentence structures in this text are quite complicated. Some of the vocabulary (*wise, studied, appeared, consulted*) would not normally be used by children not yet three. But neither of these factors seemed to deter Raja from taking over the "reading" of this story from me. The difficult vocabulary did not seem to detract from his enjoyment, and he must have been obtaining sufficient meaning, since he demanded that the book be read again and again.

A little later Raja developed a great interest in vehicles of all kinds, so we bought him Watty Piper's *Trucks* when he saw it in a book shop. Diana and I did not particularly like the book in the beginning, but it was the first one he brought us to read for about two weeks. Despite the fact that the text was expository, containing quite complex sentence structures, a lot of terminology, and a range of information that was unfamiliar to him, within the space of just over two weeks he had all 20 pages of the book under control. The following transcript indicates the nature of the text and Raja's ability to reproduce it (3.3):

> Everyone knows cars are used mainly to help people move from one place to another. Trucks, though, are used for much more. There are many kinds of trucks. Each one has a special purpose.
> A street sweeper does nothing but clean. With big brushes on its underside, it washes and sweeps the streets and gutters.

I have not used our experiences with Raja to show how clever he was at doing this. We firmly believe that all children, given similar opportunities, would be just as skillful in their use of reading-like behavior to retrieve their favorite books for themselves. Once children develop a feeling of confidence in their ability to reproduce the language of their books fluently and accurately in reading-like ways, and learn to do this with relative ease, even with new books, then they seem prepared to give more specific attention to the print.

Influencing factors

Although reading-like behavior appears to be a natural outcome of sharing books with children on a regular basis, obstacles can be placed in the path of its development. I have already mentioned the negative effects of expecting accuracy from children's attempts to participate in any shared reading. Three other factors must also be considered: book selection, the presence in the shared reading of an older brother or sister, and the way the reader reads.

Book selection

Compare the comments of two mothers who were asked if they or their children selected the books to be read together:

Mother 1: She goes through a period when she may want you to read the same book over and over again and then put it away for a month or so . . . Even when she wants a book over and over, we read it. But she doesn't bring just one book — usually four or five.

Mother 2: I usually select the stories, because I get bored very easily and I like to change the story at the end and one way of insuring that is picking them myself. Sometimes the children ask for a particular story, but I say no, I'm picking the books . . . The only exception I made was when S. was very small and he only liked a couple of stories . . . It drives me bananas to read stories that are repetitive.

The father of these last two children followed a different policy:

I'll read the book they ask for even if it's the same book again and again.

Parents have a major role to play in introducing books their children have not heard before. But if the children are to become familiar with the language of the books they want to learn to retrieve for themselves, clearly someone has to be prepared to read those stories to them again and again at their request. At least for some of the reading, the children have to feel free to select their own favorites for rereading. Actually, we are surprised at how few books we have not enjoyed, even after reading some of them literally hundreds of times.

Two conditions help overcome boredom. Over the years we were always careful in our initial selection of books to make sure they were well written, that their language "rolled off the tongue," that they were books *we* could enjoy reading. We also tried to make our readings dramatic mini-performances. Each time we read a particular book, we found ways of improving the quality of expression we brought to our reading. We experimented with different intonation patterns to bring as much meaning to the language as possible. We all enjoy doing something well. If adult readers can get rid of the hang-ups generated by their own demoralizing oral reading in school and let themselves go, they are usually surprised how much more pleasurable the experience becomes.

Older siblings

Another far less obvious barrier often occurs when two children in the same family are read to together. It is not unusual to find the older child overpowering the overt participatory actions of the younger. For example, Gillian's mother observed that Gillian's brother " . . . would not tolerate any interruptions from her." On one occasion, as I was observing their father reading to them, Gregory objected to his sister's attempts to participate in the reading on 14 separate occasions, seven for each of two books that were read. The following is an example of a transcript recorded at that time:

Father: (reading) "Oh Pooh," said Stephanie.

Gillian: (pointing to the words) That says, "Oh Pooh."

Father: (with pleasure and some surprise in his voice) That's right!

Gregory: Stop that! (Father ignores this reference to Gillian's participation and continues reading.)

The brother's interference with Gillian's overt reading-like behavior even extended to her learning the words of songs from their collection of records. She explained why she turned the volume of the stereo down very low and put her ear against the speaker:

I keep copying it when it's on. I used to put it on when we bought it. When I used to sing out loud, Greg said to me, "Stop it!" so I just had to whisper it the next time I putted it on. I had to go like this (demonstrating how she whispered).

Kaaren and Sean provided another fascinating example. Their father was reading a familiar story to them. First Kaaren and then Sean began to participate in the reading. Kaaren objected loudly to Sean's participation. The father attempted to gain some cooperation from her to allow Sean to continue to participate. Sean, meanwhile, proceeded with his attempted "reading." The following transcript is a record of the chain of events that resulted:

Sean: Once upon a time . . . (Kaaren starts shouting her protests and Sean tries again.) Once upon a time . . .

Kaaren: (shouting) I don't want to hear his [him] read! If he is going to read I read somewhere else! (The words pour out at a great rate.)

Father: (somewhat taken aback) O.K.

Kaaren: If he reads — you [the father] and me are going to go somewhere else! (Again, the words pour out.)

Father: (rather desperately) We can all read this.

Sean: (ignoring, or perhaps enjoying, all the fuss) Once upon a time . . . (Kaaren rushes from the room).

On another occasion these three were reading *The Very Hungry Caterpillar* together. Kaaren knew the story very well, much better than Sean, and every time he hesitated or miscued she would come in with the required words very quickly. On five occasions Sean cried out in considerable frustration with such protests as "Don't read!" or "Don't read with me!" or "No! Don't do it with me!" But despite his complaints and the father's several requests for Kaaren to " . . . give Sean a chance and then you can do it," she continued to dominate the shared reading until Sean finally stopped participating altogether.

Usually, however, the dominance of older children is projected in more subtle ways. Because they were participating in shared reading before their siblings' language development reached a recognizably productive stage, their continued control of the shared reading situation often goes unnoticed by parents. Because their development is more advanced and they learn more quickly the language of any new books that are being read to both children, they are almost always able to respond ahead of the younger ones.

The consequences are not always easy to determine. A great deal of reading-like behavior is going on covertly in the younger children, and for them to be forced to keep it to themselves may not necessarily be harmful to their reading development. In Gillian's case, for example, her father commented that:

She's just a much more passive kind of person in the reading process, I think, than Greg was . . . Gillian is the kind of person who takes it all in and surprises you. All of a sudden, she lays it all out.

What the father did not consider was the strong possibility that Gillian's passivity may have been a direct result of her brother's dominance. But despite his overwhelming of her overt participation, she still managed to develop an amazing amount of control over the language of her books.

Sometimes, however, the control is pervasive and persistent to the point where the younger child regularly seeks alternative activities. Rather than try to compete with the older brother or sister, or be forced to play an entirely passive role, the child is happy to seek other means of personally controlled enjoyment. In that case, damage may well be done to reading development. Because parents do not understand why the child quickly and consistently leaves the shared reading, they often misinterpret the behavior as an indication that he or she has little or no interest in books and reading. They provide more alternative play activities instead, and may not even buy that child as many books.

As Kaaren's father found out, it is not easy to reduce or eliminate the older child's dominant role in the shared reading situation. If time is available, each child can be read to separately, but if and when the family grows larger, this becomes more difficult. It is possible, however, to allow each child to select a particular book, and when that story is being read, the other child must remain silent and leave any participation to the one whose book it is. The problem is at least partially resolved when the older child goes off to school and the younger one can have the all-important undivided attention of the parents for some of the time.

The reader's style

Children use a variety of strategies to learn to reproduce their stories, described earlier in this chapter as *mumble, completion, echo* and *cooperative* reading. The use of these strategies develops intuitively, but their growth may be markedly influenced by the way the stories are read. Where the reader reads too quickly or does not pause at appropriate points to invite participation, the amount of overt participation is severely restricted.

Linguists have established that we comprehend best when we listen to language that is being produced at our own rate. The most appropriate speed at which to read would appear to be one that approximates the child's own rate of speech. From my observations of shared reading situations, *mumble* and *cooperative* reading are encouraged when the reader's reading rate is slower, or at least no faster than that of the children's spoken language.

Completion reading is facilitated by the skill of the reader in knowing when (and how long) to pause as an invitation to the children to "close the gap" and complete the phrase or sentence. No one can tell a reader when or how long to pause during the reading of a familiar story. This has to be learned by trial and error. Sometimes children begin completing lines during the very first reading. At other times, despite the fact that they could reproduce the whole story for themselves with the utmost ease, they prefer to sit and listen without participating at all. The reader has to develop an acute sense of timing to ensure the children's continued participation in joyful and successful ways.

While *mumble, cooperative* and *completion* reading are used without any conscious effort on the part of the children (and often the reader), *echo* reading is sometimes specifically suggested or requested. For example, at 5.11 Gillian started to use this strategy, apparently to gain control over a new book as quickly as possible. Her mother recorded in the "Reading Diary" she had been maintaining for me:

> April 24
>
> She dragged out *Button Soup* to read again. We did half the story together. She read each sentence after me.
>
> April 26
>
> . . . then we read the second half of *Button Soup*. She read each sentence after me. Took a while, but she insisted on completing the task she set for herself.

When I visited the home shortly after these entries, Gillian brought me the same book, opened it and issued the following instructions:

> But first you've got to read — hmm — this, then I have to — and then when you've finished, I have to read after you.

I proceeded to read in the manner she suggested and we continued to *echo* read the whole book, although at times she took over from me completely. At one point, after she had "read" a section, she paused and I expected her to continue. However, with an emphatic "Go ahead!" I was ordered to resume my lead role. It was not difficult to know who was controlling the learning process!

Conclusion

Children can and will participate freely in the shared reading of favorite stories, provided we facilitate their participation through the way we read to them. We have to view the process as one of genuine shared learning and, just as we take turns when we talk with our children, we should encourage in every possible way the taking of turns during our reading of books. We constantly invite children to engage in conversations with us, and enjoy their approximating efforts. We should do the same when we invite them to share their books with us.

Under these supportive conditions, books and reading become an integral and productive part of children's lives, contributing constantly to their need to involve themselves in creative, meaning-making activities. The language of books

— its authenticity, its power to convey thought and meaning, and its undoubted potential for making a substantial contribution to the children's fragile but fertile imaginations — provides a source of learning that is available in no other way. Reproducing that language with all its richness, variety and color, in intonationally alive ways, gives children an opportunity to respond with a depth of understanding not likely to be achieved otherwise. Their power as language users is greatly enhanced, their knowledge of the real and the "unreal" world considerably enlarged, and their ability to generate thoughts and images without reference to the here and now vastly extended.

Children who are read to regularly by their parents and teachers are being given what they are entitled to in a society that expects them to become fully literate. When they are invited and encouraged to participate in the reading in reading-like ways, their development as fluent readers is virtually assured. All that is required for them to become independent readers is the opportunity to continue the process of learning to read in natural and self-directed ways as they begin to understand how to use the print on the page.

Gaining control over print

Children can generate very positive and powerful attitudes towards books and reading. They can also learn to reproduce the language and meaning of their books with surprising ease and increasing accuracy. But can they continue to learn to read in this self-directed manner? Can they take the next step and learn to read what has not been read to them? Can they work out for themselves how to use print as one of the three main cueing systems to help them read new stories? In other words, having gained considerable control over the non-visual systems in retrieving their favorite stories, can they now direct their attention to the visual for help in their effort to become independent readers? Even more importantly, can they learn to use the visual cueing system without having it become the dominant source of information as they read?

In the studies of early readers, most of the children who "taught" themselves to read constantly asked questions about written language and how it worked, and the answers they were given were usually simple, direct and, most significantly, immediate. But few of them had ever received formal instruction concerning how to use print in the process of reading. How had they managed to master this seemingly complex and demanding task more or less on their own?

I repeat, in order for children to gain independent access to books that have not been read to them, they must first have a compelling desire to do so. They must also be firmly convinced that the stories being read to them are contained in the print on the pages of their books, not somehow coming "out of the heads" of those who read them. Until this need is present and this understanding is part of their conscious knowledge about how reading "works," children are likely to remain quite happily dependent on others for their reading experiences.

Although it is possible to describe some of the conditions that contribute to these important developments, as well as the behaviors that indicate they are occurring, it is not possible to say when they will occur. The extent, range, type and quality of the children's previous experiences with written language will play a major part, of course. But just as important will be whether the environment in which they have been growing up has nurtured risk-taking attitudes and a willingness to do things independently.

The desire for independence

The realization that they *can* read is a necessary condition for children to formulate the explicit desire to learn to read independently. Jennifer's mother recorded the following observation in her Reading Diary about Jennifer (3.3):

Only a while ago she realized that children could read too. Up till then she thought only adults could read the words. I brought a little friend of hers over one afternoon — Nicky, who is in grade four — and she sat down and read a whole pile of books. Before that she was convinced that children didn't read, only big people did.

Children like Jennifer, who do not have older brothers or sisters who can read, may persist in seeing reading as an adult task, at least until they go to school. The growth of an intrinsically motivated drive towards achieving independence as a reader may therefore also be delayed.

In Gillian's case, this drive did not begin to show itself in any recognizable form until she was around 5.6. Until that time, she seemed comfortable with her well-developed ability to retrieve her numerous familiar stories through the use of fluent reading-like behavior. Like Kaaren, Sean and Jennifer, she was secure in her view that, along with hearing the stories being read, seeing the pictures played the most important part in reading. I asked Kaaren (4.8) how she knew what to say when she was "reading" her stories, and she observed:

> Because you can see the pictures. If there weren't even pictures you won't know what the word says — *not even if you have glasses* [her emphasis].

7-20

"How's anybody s'posed to read these books of yours? There are no pictures in 'em!"

I once read a book to Gillian (5.4) and asked her how she thought I had managed to learn to read. The following conversation took place:

Gillian: 'Cause you listen to the words.

David: Do I read the words or listen to the words?

Gillian: Listen to the words.

Gillian's views became even more apparent when we were talking about reading generally one day. She commented, with honest conviction, that she could "teach" her cat and dog to read. I was intrigued (and surprised) by her remark, so I asked her her how she might do that.

David: Teach your cat and dog to read?

Gillian: Yeah! 'Cause Smokey [her dog] — I — when I ask her to — when I say "Smokey!" she just — she just sits. And I say "Smokey!" (As if giving the dog an order.)

David: But is she learning to read if you do that? Is she reading? (Two different questions, unfortunately.)

Gillian: (uncertainly) No.

David: Do you think Smokey can learn to read these words?

Gillian: (with considerable emphasis) If I only tell her!

Not only could Gillian learn to read by hearing words read to her over and over again, but because the animals had demonstrated an ability to understand oral language in the form of orders, they too could learn to read. All Gillian had to do to teach them was say the words over and over again!

When I asked Gillian, approximately two months later, if she wished she could read all the words in her stories, she produced a very meaningful sigh, accompanied by a drawn-out and wishful "Yeah!" I then asked her why, and although her response is not fully decipherable on the tape, it sounds as if she was saying she was dissatisfied with being constantly dependent on having stories read to her before she could read them for herself. Like the little boy who lamented to Marie Clay when "reading" one of his familiar stories: "I wish I could really truly read this book for myself," Gillian was beginning to feel a sense of frustration at her continued dependence on others.

When I asked her one month later if she thought she could read, she replied with an ambivalent "No — yeah." Gillian was beginning to exhibit some uncertainty. After she had finished "reading" one of her favorite stories, the following conversation took place when I asked her whether she was reading:

Gillian: Hm. Hmm (with an upward "yes" inflection).

David: What are you doing?

Gillian: Pointing to the words.

David: So you're reading? Are you reading when you're doing that?

Gillian: Well, not very much (in a resigned tone of voice).

David: Not very much?

Gillian: Nope. Not very much.

Clearly, she was beginning to realize that there is more to reading than simply reproducing the language and meaning of stories in reading-like ways. Her attitude altered quite dramatically in a short time. Her mother recorded in her Reading Diary that Gillian (5.9) was beginning to hold quite a different opinion about the nature of the task. One day, as the two of them listened to some new stories on tape, following along in the accompanying books, Gillian observed quite seriously that she was " . . . not interested in learning to read. It's too much work!"

A month later, I asked her again if she could "read with her eyes closed." She replied with a firm "No!" and stated the reason with equal firmness: " 'Cause you can't see the words."

"But," I probed, "you were able to read your *My Big Book of Pretty Pussies* with your eyes closed."

Gillian replied, "Yes. But that's because I knew the verses well." Obviously she now knew the difference between her "reading" and "real" reading.

The next month, prompted by what her mother had written in the Reading Diary, I again asked Gillian if she thought learning to read would be easy or hard for her. She replied emphatically:

Gillian: Hard!

David: Why is it going to be hard?

Gillian: Because I don't know very much words.

David: But you know a lot of words.

Gillian: I know, except — you know — 'munication and stuff like that. I don't even know how to spell communication!

It was clear that she believed at this stage that in order to learn to read she had to remember what every word in every book looked like so she could recognize each one as she tried to read independently. Since she had been trying to do this without the kind of success she had experienced in learning to reproduce her favorite stories through reading-like behavior, she had begun to see the process of learning to read with different eyes.

8-15

"Neither of us can read yet."

Some of the entries in her mother's Reading Diary for this period help us see Gillian's change of attitude. Words had obviously assumed great importance for her. These entries also provide us with some understanding of how she had decided to continue the process of learning to read.

March 31
Tonight more stories from their Bible Book . . . Gill. went through the first story locating words she knows — as, God, the, etc.

April 2
She initiated the reading of a prayer in one story. Went through (pointing with her finger) pointing out all the words she recognized. I assisted with others which she recognized on a second appearance.

April 11
Picked up a book this a.m. and proceeded to read out all the words she knew.

May 23
Gill. dragged out about 8 to 10 Disney books to read by herself this a.m., asking me the difficult words. She continues to read instead of memorizing.

May 25
She bounced out of bed early today (8 a.m.) and proceeded to read two books to me . . . She read *Whose Mouse Are You?* and *Where the Wild Things Are*, spelling out any words she didn't know and asked what they were. She's actually reading, isn't she?

May 27
At breakfast today Gill. read *Morris the Moose* with help from Greg. [her brother] again. She's definitely reading each word — looks very intent.

Gillian's change of attitude towards reading and her expressed opinion that it would involve "too much work" did not alter her drive to master the task for herself. Her persistent attempts to read her stories by "staying with the print" demonstrated that, like Laura Beth, she was quite determined to work her way through her familiar books, to see for herself if she could read them by "remembering the words." When she became stuck, she sought, and received, immediate assistance from her mother or brother. The concentrated attention she was giving to the learning process gave no indication that she saw it as "too much work."

It is obvious that Gillian's years of intensely pleasurable and meaningful book experiences were sustaining an inner compulsion to gain mastery over the process of reading, no matter how difficult she saw this task to be. Increasingly, she was not waiting to be invited to share in the reading of her books, but openly demanding control. Her mother told me how, when they were sharing the reading of one of her newly learned stories, Gillian (5.9) would take over the reading with a peremptory, "Don't tell me! Don't tell me!" When she came to a word she did not know she would ask for help, but then would say immediately, "Now don't tell me any more!"

Although she believed at this stage that learning to read involved learning to recognize all the words by remembering what each one looked like, the overwhelming complexity of the task did not dissuade her from wanting to try. The hundreds of joyful hours she had spent in the company of her books, the confident control she had been able to generate over the language of these books, her growing knowledge of print and how it works, and her explicitly formulated drive to want to read independent of others kept her at the task. As we will see in the next section of this chapter, her wide-ranging experience with written language in its many forms contributed significantly to her growing knowledge about the essential role of print in reading.

The role of print

Today's children live in an environment that literally bombards them with print: road signs, billboards, fast food signs, supermarket notices, restaurant menus and TV ads, for example. Unless children are physically impaired by the loss of hearing or vision, they cannot avoid learning to associate some written symbols with the language they hear and see being used so functionally around them every day.

Children who live in a literacy-oriented home easily become aware of specific features and purposes of written language. Sometimes, parents instinctively run their fingers underneath the lines of print. Sometimes, they point to featured words or ask the children to turn the page. They point to and read the titles of the stories and their authors' names, and make comments such as "Here's where we start reading" and "That's the end of the story." All these contribute to the children's growing awareness of the presence of print on the pages of their books. Their book-handling knowledge and their general curiosity about how written language works develop quite naturally through opportunities to make books an integral part of their lives.

These children see their parents engaged in writing as well. They see their own names printed and written on numerous occasions and for a variety of purposes. Grocery lists and messages for family members or friends are recorded in their presence, with simple explanations concerning their purpose and use. Birthday cards, invitations, Christmas cards and letters to relatives are composed, and the children add their own messages and names. Letters and invitations addressed to them cause great excitement and are often carried around for days. Communicating through written language is a perfectly natural thing for these children, and they will want to learn to write for themselves.

Sensitive parents invite and encourage them to write by providing crayons, pencils, ballpoints, felt pens, suitable paper — and a place to use and store them. They support with praise the children's approximating and experimental efforts and display them proudly in prominent places. They send letters "written" to relatives, including whatever translation may be necessary and a request for a reply. The children may also try their hand at writing their own stories, perhaps modeling their efforts on the examples provided by their favorite authors. Judith Newman, in *The Craft of Children's Writing* (1984), has described simply and clearly how young children develop as writers when they are provided with the appropriate conditions for doing so.

Among the first signs that children are beginning to take an interest in the print in their books are questions like "Where does it say that?" or "What is that word?" When these questions arise as stories are being read, it is apparent that the child has reached an extremely important stage as a reader. The print on the page is starting to have some significance. The path to becoming an independent reader is becoming more clearly defined.

Too often we assume that young children learn very easily what words and letters are and what their roles are in written language. All we have to do is tell or show them the differences between letters and words and they will then understand what letters and words are and how they are used. And if we repeatedly demonstrate to them how certain letters "make certain sounds" (as *Sesame Street* does, for example), then they should be able to store this information away, learn all the symbol-to-sound relationships and pronounce any word they see, through a process of "sounding out."

But children do not learn about letters and words and the role they have in writing and reading *by being told about them*. They must generate these abstract and complex understandings for themselves, as the result of a wide variety of experiences with written language used in highly functional and meaningful ways. And such concepts take time to form. Children may quickly learn the names of the letters through the repeated use of alphabet books, blocks, magnetized letters and the like, but it may be several years before they understand that letters and words serve different purposes in written language. Letter-name knowledge is useful in talking about written language and in learning to write, but it has a relatively minor role to play in learning to read.

Learning that the recording of print on the pages of books follows certain conventions, and that the stories they hear are preserved on these pages, through print, in a predictable manner are difficult and abstract understandings for young children to develop. Knowing that print goes from left to right and down the page in a linear fashion is learned early and easily, but realizing that each word is separated by white spaces, and that letters and words are not the same, places far greater demands on children.

Even more difficult for them to learn are sound-symbol relationships. The sounds they hear in words are represented by entirely different letters or sets of letters in different words (for example, *tough* and *stuff*). Or the same letters can represent quite different sounds (for example, *moon* and *book*, *Sam* and *same*). Sometimes it is only meaning that determines how a word sounds (for example, "tomorrow I will *read* this book" and "yesterday I *read* that book"). To expect children to consciously and constructively master the vast range of generalizations that need to be learned in order to rely solely on print information for reading a book independently is expecting the impossible. Just as they are able to develop, without any formal instruction, an intuitive control over the grammar necessary for composing syntactically acceptable sentences while talking, so too, if given the opportunity, they will develop control over the ways written language is composed — as early readers and writers have been demonstrating for decades, probably for centuries.

It *takes time* to develop the knowledge and understanding that children need in order to use the extensive range of important concepts about print and sound-symbol relationships in a systematic manner while reading independently. Their development bears a direct relationship to the quality and quantity of experience the children have with written language. Their often random exploration of print, their natural curiosity, their constant desire to know more about "those black marks" on the page, and their compelling drive to achieve independence keep them at the task. Provided control of the learning process is left in their hands, they will continue to make progress in working it all out for themselves.

From the age of about 3, Gillian could print her own name and recognize it among other words. On request, she could isolate words and letters in a line of print and point to the first and last letters in a word. She knew all the letter names of the alphabet and could match these names to the printed form of the letters in either upper or lower case. Her finger-matching of word-space-word when someone read to her was usually perfect. She had even begun to use initial letters and other visual clues to identify words as she was reproducing some of her favorite stories. At 5.4 she could recognize a large number of words at sight. She had a growing writing vocabulary which she used, with her mother's help, to write letters and a variety of cards to friends. Clearly, Gillian had learned a great deal about written language and how it is composed.

But despite her knowledge of the form and function of print, Gillian still insisted that she could read with her eyes closed. She was also convinced that the way to learn to read was to listen to someone read a story repeatedly until she was able to reproduce it for herself — without looking at the words. When asked to count the number of words in a line of print, she would often persist in counting the letters, no matter how clearly the request was made. Perhaps even more surprising, when shown a line of print without any spaces between the words, she could detect nothing unusual or different about it. Yet when asked to find the words *vanilla ice cream* in that line, she did so immediately, still quite certain that there was nothing unusual about the print. Although she had learned a lot about print and was beginning to use it frequently in her reading and writing, her knowledge had apparently not come together to the point where she could use it consistently, accurately and with conviction.

By the time she was close to 6, however, much of her knowledge had indeed "come together." She had become convinced of the importance of using the print while reading. As we will see in the next section of this chapter, having access to large amounts of print which she could examine at her leisure provided her with a very functional platform from which she could launch herself into independence in reading.

Arhythmic reading-like behavior

Movement from the fluent reproduction of favorite stories to a slower, more arhythmic reading-like behavior signifies a major development in children's progress in learning to read. No longer are they convinced that the illustrations and what is in the reader's head control what is read. They are beginning to realize that what they are saying as they retrieve their stories for themselves can be matched with what they are seeing in the print on the pages. They may stop for quite long periods of time as they inspect a word visually, even though they could say the word correctly and quickly if they were to revert to a fluent reconstruction of the text. No one has to tell them to move to this mode of reading. The change happens quite spontaneously.

Learning to eye-ear-voice match

Although adults find it a simple task to point accurately to the words they read, the process is often fraught with difficulties for children when they commence to "voice point," a process that slows down their reading. Sometimes exact matches cannot be made because they have not mastered an accurate reproduction of the story being read at the word level. Usually, though, they seem to know which stories they know well enough to read arhythmically.

Frequently, as the following transcripts show, the major problem occurs when they try to achieve an exact match with multisyllabic words. Because they enunciate each word very carefully, they say each syllable as a separate word. For example, if the word has three syllables, they point to the word as they say the first syllable, then to the next two words as they pronounce the final two syllables. This, of course, causes them to run out of words to point to. They usually know enough about the visual information available in the print to realize they have lost their place, and they often stop trying to eye-ear-voice match in sheer frustration, reverting to fluent reading where little notice is taken of the print.

The first short transcript, which reveals the nature of the multisyllabic problem, was recorded by Judith Newman on videotape as part of a research project we were conducting jointly into early literacy development in Nova Scotia. Bobby (5.9) had volunteered to read Bill Martin's *Brown Bear, Brown Bear*, stating that he wanted to "read the whole thing." He immediately adopted an arhythmic style and pointed to the words with everything at his disposal: his head, his voice and his finger. But when he came to the "redbird" page, he struck trouble, since on this page the name of the animal is written as one word while the rest are written as two (brown bear, yellow duck, blue horse, etc.). The words Bobby pointed to in the text are underlined:

Text	Bobby
<u>Redbird</u>	Red
<u>Redbird</u>	bird
<u>What do</u> you see?	Red — bird — aw! (Stops pointing, exhibits confusion, returns to the beginning and starts again, reading even more slowly and deliberately.)
<u>Redbird</u>	Red
<u>Redbird</u>	bird
<u>What do</u> you see?	Red — bird (Stops pointing, pauses.) That doesn't say "Red"! (Points to *What*, demonstrating considerable frustration.)

It was clear that Bobby had learned enough about sound-to-letter relationships to know that *What* did not say *Red*, but he did not know how his dilemma had arisen, nor how to resolve it. Judith offered her assistance, which he readily accepted. She read the page again slowly, pointing accurately as she did so, but offered no explanation as to what the problem was, preferring to leave him to work it out for himself. He continued to read in an arhythmic manner, experiencing only one further difficulty when he accidentally missed out a whole page. He knew once again that something was wrong, since what he was seeing did not match what he wanted to say, sought help again, obtained it quickly and proceeded through to the end of the book, exhibiting quiet satisfaction and considerable pleasure over his substantial accomplishment.

Gillian began to experience similar problems with her matching as she engaged in retrieving her stories through the use of arhythmic reading-like behavior (5.7):

Text	Gillian
<u>I was sitting in</u> a tankard one day	I — was — sit — ting (Stops pointing and reading.) No!

I̲ was̲ sitting̲ in̲ a̲ tankard̲ one̲ day	I-was-sitting-in-a — tan — kard-one (Stops pointing and reading and starts from tankard again.)
tankard̲ one̲ day̲ (Points twice to day.)	tan — kard-one-day
Just biding my time, (Does not finger point, voice points.)	Just-passing-my-time,

She continued to read part of the next line in this voice-pointing manner until I prompted her, when she became stuck, by rereading the lines fluently and then pausing for her to take over. She did so, and continued to read the remainder of the page in a fluent manner.

Looking at the transcript, we see that Gillian was able to overcome the matching problem she experienced with *sitting in* satisfactorily, but could not resolve the one with *tankard one day*. Since the word *in* was one she could recognize at sight, it would seem that she realized when she said "ting" and pointed to *in* that something was not right. She took a rerun at this part of the line and matched her finger with the words up to *tankard one day*. Her careful enunciation of "tan-kard" caused her to point to *one* as she said "-kard." At this point she realized she had two more words to say but only one to point to. She took a rerun at it from the word *tankard*, again treating it as two words. This time, however, she continued to the end of the line, resolving the problem simply by pointing twice to the word *day* to compensate for her error in matching. She then abandoned finger-pointing, later giving as her reason "'Cause when I point I get all mixed up!" But she continued to read in a voice-pointing manner until my modeling seemed to prompt her to revert to fluent reading, in which she gave little or no attention to the visual information available to her.

Building phonic knowledge

Like Laura Beth, Gillian reproduced a great many of her favorite books in this way. Children at this stage of their development seem to know instinctively that by matching exactly what they are saying with what they are seeing in the print on the pages of their books they can learn to read independently. By using large chunks of written language that is very familiar to them, they build their knowledge of this source of information. *By constantly going from the sound of known words to their visual representation, they are in a position to generate their own rule system for the complex range of relationships used to compose words out of letters.* As Frank Smith so aptly reminds us, "Phonics are easy if you already have a good idea what the word is in the first place" (1983).

Learning "phonic" relationships through words they already know within the context and flow of intensely meaningful language makes this learning possible. The *sequence* of their learning (based on their previously developed knowledge), the *content* of their learning (based on what they decide they need to know at any particular time in order to continue reading), and the *decision* as to what parts of the words to examine in order to confirm or to disprove any predictions all come from the children themselves. Like the building of their grammars for the production of meaningful spoken language, the construction of their rule system for the sound-to-letter(s) and letter(s)-to-sound relationships in written language remains under their control and continues to grow at their rate.

Learning their "phonic rules system" can be accelerated if they are experimenting with writing at the same time, since they will be thinking through the sound-to-symbol patterns as they attempt to record them in print. Playing word and letter games with them (finding all the words that start with the first letter of their names, looking for similarities and differences in words), finding word families, and generally drawing attention to notable features in written language in incidental and enjoyable ways can also help speed up the process of understanding how written language is recorded.

Developing control over eye movements

Using arhythmic reading-like behavior provides children with the opportunity to develop additional abilities important in the process of reading and writing. For example, they learn quite naturally to establish control over the intricate eye movements so necessary for fluent reading. Without any conscious effort on their part, they learn to run their eyes along a line of print in a series of saccadic (hopping) movements at a rate suited to their own needs and purposes. They also learn to move their eyes down the page, line by line, using an accurate return sweep to hit the first word in the next line.

They learn intuitively to make fewer and fewer pauses, of shorter and shorter duration, and to use as little of the visual information as possible to confirm the predictions they make based on their knowledge of the structure and meaning of the language they are reading. Unless children have a great deal of self-directed practice of this kind, their development as fluent readers will be delayed until their control over the fine motor coordination needed to make rhythmic eye movements has been established. The lack of "visual control," so often detected in non-fluent readers of all ages, is almost certainly the outcome of being forced to inspect every word very carefully, stopping frequently to sound them out.

Stretching words out

During arhythmic reading, children enunciate the words of their stories very clearly and carefully. They stretch the words out, thereby developing their ear for the sound (phonemic) units within them. Not only does this contribute to their growing ability to inspect words and their parts more carefully, it seems to be a foundational skill for learning to spell, initially as the words sound, then conventionally. It is quite probable that many of the children who experience difficulty learning to spell accurately never had the opportunity to go through this stage of carefully enunciating the words of familiar stories, phonemic unit by phonemic unit. They have, in fact, never learned to hear the sound units within words distinctly.

Conclusion

Learning to use the visual information as an integral and essential, *but not dominant*, part of the process of reading does not (and should not) occur as an isolated learning task for children. It is dependent on their skilled use of book language. It is intimately related to the growth of their desire to learn to read independently and to their belief that they can learn to read just as adults do. As their awareness of print and of the conventions that regulate its recording develops, so also does the attention they are prepared to give to them. A major step has been taken in their drive to gain independent access to books.

There is still a lot to learn, but as long as control of that learning remains where it belongs, in the children's receptive and active hands, learning will continue with few interruptions. The information-processing centers of their absorbent brains will not become overloaded and failure-inducing bottlenecks will occur rarely. Learning to read will continue as an entirely successful and intensely pleasurable activity to be engaged in at will. The gates to the world of books are close to being opened; the keys to those gates are turning more and more easily in their locks. All that remains is for the children to put it all together, to orchestrate fully the knowledge and skill that have been nurtured so naturally over the preceding years.

Putting it all together

First let me restate the basic assumption that underlies the theory described in this book: *If children are to grow up learning to read as naturally as they learn to talk, they have to grow up in a literacy-oriented environment.* Parents, teachers, relatives and friends have to be readers, constantly displaying their "addiction" to reading through their own sustained devouring of books and various other kinds of written language. Avid readers cannot resist going to books, opening their covers and sampling their pages. Unlike the harmful effects of most other addictions, however, reading is usually joyously generative and uplifting.

Copyright 1979
2-5
The Register and Tribune
Syndicate, Inc.

**. . . Then little Claire followed Glenny Gopher
into the woods and. . . ."**

But a rich literacy environment contains more than just avid readers; it is filled with written materials of all kinds. It provides access to "the right book for the right time" — books that invite and demand attention, that once started cannot be put down; books that provide the framework for that inner dialogue between author and reader so important for the expansion of the human mind; books that stimulate the imagination, provide flights of fantasy and paths to new ways of thinking. The growth of a reader requires that the roots be supplied with an uninterrupted flow of appropriate nutrients. To expect healthy, self-regulated reading growth to occur without providing the necessary conditions is unrealistic and naive.

When children are willing and able to reproduce their favorite books by "staying with the print," they are just about on their own as readers. Although parents and teachers should continue to read to them on a regular basis, adding a steady flow of new books and authors to the old favorites, the children will be spending increasing amounts of time reading on their own. Now the adults have another important role to play. They have to make sure that the young readers they are "growing" are supplied with the two basic requirements: appropriate nutrients (authentic literature) and sufficient sunlight (time and space to enjoy it).

Orchestrating the visual and non-visual information

It is a major theme of this book that almost any intervention by others in a skills-teaching, instructional sense will interfere with the multi-dimensional, simultaneous processing of print we call reading. All too often, instruction will cause the reader to focus attention on *one* aspect of the process to the exclusion of other, perhaps more important, ones.

Instead, children have to pace *themselves* as learners, as an outcome of their intrinsically motivated determination to become independent. Any help offered must support that motivation and determination, not undermine it. Our attempts to assist the process have to facilitate self-directed learning rather than impose what we think needs to be learned. The model we should follow is the one we use instinctively in promoting growth in oral language learning: immersion, demonstration and the opportunity for the children to experiment and approximate in their efforts to learn.

The process of gaining control over print by orchestrating the use of the available visual and non-visual information seems to follow a natural progression. Children first use their most familiar stories to read in a voice-pointing or arhythmic manner. They are able to reproduce these with a high degree of confidence at the word level, which leaves them free to concentrate their attention on learning to match word-space-word and to build their knowledge of the complex array of patterns and relationships among letters that are used to represent words.

Once they gain control over the matching process, they take the next step and try their hand at reading less familiar books. After new stories have been read to them only once or twice, they start to take over the reading and begin to reproduce them with a *mixture* of fluent and arhythmic reading, sometimes seeking help from anyone available, but mostly working it out for themselves.

Gillian (5.11) received a new book from the Disney Book Club entitled *Button Soup*. After echo reading it twice with her mother, she proceeded to share it with me. Gradually, she started going beyond the words I had read, reading parts independently. Finally, she stopped me altogether with the highly significant comment, "I think I can read it now." The following brief transcript shows how she did it:

Text	Gillian
"You won't find any food around here," he said.	(Reads fluently.) "You won't find any food . . . No! That's food. (Rereads this, voice pointing very carefully.) "You — won't — find — any — food — around — h — here," — he — said.
He tried to hide some dirty dishes.	(Reads fluently.) He tried to hide some dirty dishes. (Rereads, but this time voice points for the first part of the sentence.) He — tried — to — hide — some dirty dishes.

It seems probable that, even though she read the first line fluently, Gillian was still looking at the print. Her eyes were moving ahead of her voice, which is what normally happens when we read fluently orally. She then realized that what she was saying did not match what she was seeing ("No! That's food.") and reverted to arhythmic reading so she could eye-ear-voice match with absolute accuracy. Having satisfied herself that she could read it, she switched back to fluent reading for the next line. But then she did something that was extremely interesting: *she reread this section, voice-pointing very carefully until she was satisfied she had been reading accurately*, then finished up reading the last three words fluently. She continued to read the remainder of the book in this manner, pausing only occasionally to seek my assistance with a word and demonstrating quiet satisfaction over her considerable achievement.

This short transcript provides us with a lovely example of a young girl taking control of the learning-to-read process for herself and, quite deliberately, trying herself out on a relatively unfamiliar story. When she thinks she is off course, she stops, runs a more careful check on the visual information, satisfies herself that what she is saying is indeed correct, and goes on. By switching in and out of fluent and arhythmic reading, she provides herself with sustained opportunities to learn to use all three cueing systems available to her in whatever ratio she needs. Almost certainly, she is learning that she needs to use only minimal amounts of the visual information to confirm the predictions she has made on the basis of her knowledge of language and meaning.

On my last research visit to Gillian's home, I read Maurice Sendak's *Where the Wild Things Are* with her. She was almost six by this time. I had helped her select the book from the public library and had read it to her twice, with her participating in some of the repetitive parts (for example, *And they rolled their terrible eyes*). At her request, we began to read it for the third time. She participated in a cooperative manner, reading along with me and sometimes taking the lead. Suddenly, she interrupted me and, using her most authoritative tone, said, "You've got to let me read now!" Here is a transcript of part of her reading (Gillian's deviations from the original text have been underlined wherever possible):

Text	**Gillian**
The night Max wore his wolf suit	The night when Max (pauses and self-corrects) . . . the night Max wore his wolf suit
and made mischief of one kind and another,	making a mischief of one kind and another,
his mother called him wild thing.	his mother called him the wild thing.
And Max said, "I'll eat you up!"	And Max said, "I'm going to eat you up!" (Read with tremendous emphasis.)
So he was sent to bed without eating anything.	So Max went (self-corrects) . . . so he went to bed without eating anything.
That night in Max's room a jungle grew,	That very (points to *night* and asks "What does that say?" but before she can be told, she rereads, self-corrects and begins to voice point) . . . that night — in — Max's — room — a — forest — grew (pauses and self-corrects) — a — jungle — grew. (When asked how she knew that the word was *jungle* and not *forest* she pointed to the *f* in *forest* and said, "That's not a "juh," it's a "fuh.")

Gillian read the rest of the book in this manner, pausing occasionally to ask what a word was and then, before I could respond, saying it correctly herself, frequently after rereading the part of the text just before the word. What miscues she made were almost always of high quality. She read confidently, expressively and fluently, occasionally reverting to arhythmic reading to run a more careful check on the visual information. Since this was only the third time the book had been read with her, it was not possible for her to have memorized all the words. In a very real sense, she was now using all the strategies employed by competent, adult readers, despite the fact that her graphophonic knowledge was not fully developed. Most significantly, she was in control of her own learning, monitoring her performance and self-correcting when she felt it was necessary.

Gillian continued her drive towards independent reading. Her mother reported that almost every morning before breakfast she would take a collection of books to the couch in the living room and read them, seeking help whenever she needed it. The books ranged from old favorites to recently acquired ones that had been read together only a few times. Like Laura Beth, she would read to herself, to her dolls and stuffed animals, and to anyone who would listen. When she was rereading very familiar text, she was seen to lapse into silent reading on occasion. She found that her mouth could not keep up with her mind, so she simply stopped reading orally. When a new set of library books was brought home, or when a new issue of her children's magazine or her latest book club book arrived, Gillian would immediately try her hand at reading them. The magazine was a particularly rich source of risk-taking for her, since she was very interested in its games and puzzles and worked at reading the instructions for them assiduously. As soon as she had found out what to do, she would call on someone to share in the fun. Her new-found independence was being put to use!

Neither Gillian's nor Laura Beth's parents could pinpoint the moment when their daughters — or their slightly older sons, Gregory and Christopher, who were both reading before they went to school — became independent readers. But once all these children knew they could read stories without first having to hear them, they began devouring new books at a great rate and at every available opportunity, as if to demonstrate to themselves that they were now fully independent. Just as children who have recently learned to walk seek, even demand, the chance to try out their newly learned skill, so do young readers who are flexing their reading muscles go to books as often as possible. It is easy to see why our homes and schools should be flooded with books of all kinds — so those developing readers need only reach out to find new risks to take, new challenges to meet, new vistas to explore.

Regaining fluency

Having reached this stage of independence, children begin to work at learning to read new stories with the same kind of fluency they possessed when they "read" their old favorites. Their store of immediately recognized words increases and they begin to use the remembered features of known words when they examine new words with similar features. Their intuitively developed knowledge of the patterns and relationships between the sounds of words and word parts and their visual representation continues to grow as they reread old favorites arhythmically.

Their efforts to produce written language in their writing provides them with another avenue for checking out what they know about print. They constantly experiment with this knowledge as they endeavor to read new stories, testing their established hypotheses. They stretch out the unknown word, listening carefully to see if it checks with what makes sense and sounds like language, trying to confirm their prediction of what it might be. They reread the phrase or sentence before an unknown word to re-establish the syntactic and semantic cohesion of the text. Sometimes, they simply leave the word out, perhaps returning to it later after having worked out what it is from the additional information obtained by reading on. If they are real risk-takers, they will substitute another word that makes sense within the context of the story. When none of these strategies seems to work, they seek help from anyone who is available at the time. They have developed a highly functional range of ways to deal with any difficulties they may meet.

Harmful strategies

There are a variety of ways to help children with words they are unable to recognize. Telling them the word is the simplest, of course, but it carries a potentially harmful effect. Once we commence "helping" readers this way, we run the danger of making them into dependent learners — the very opposite of what we want to promote. If we do it every time, we soon find that they begin to wait longer and longer for our help. Instead of providing them with an opportunity to try out their own strategies, or modeling some they might use, we deny them the chance to learn to experiment and grow as independent readers.

The instruction to "sound it out" is, unfortunately, too often the only help children are given. It is, in fact, one of the most confusing and confounding strategies to direct children to use. By encouraging, and often compelling, them to use this technique, we cause them to focus all their attention on small segments of the visual information available to them. We thus distract them from more useful cues, such as their knowledge of language and meaning *in association with* what they know about letter-sound relationships.

Let us take the word *honest,* one that Frank Smith uses to draw attention to "the fallacy of phonics." Listen to the sound of the letter *o* as you say "ho," "hon," "hone," "hones" and then "honest" — or should it be "onest"? Where did the *h* go? Without it, you might even say "wunst" ("one-st"). What do you have to know about the relationships between letters in words to know what sounds you should be making, how you should group the letters, and what range of sounds those letters could make?

Now make a list of words starting with a consonant-vowel pattern and try sounding them out, remembering that you already know what the words are and that you have established your phonic rule system through years of experience involving a tremendous amount of trial and error. Or have someone make up a list of words like the following, without showing them to you: *do, does, dose, don't, doubt, door, doom, double, dolphin* and *doily*. Then have that person present those words to you, uncovering the letters one at a time as you sound them out. Perhaps you could manage the task better if you went from right-to-left rather than left-to-right!

Now try to sound out *those* and *thing*. Can you hear the voiced th sound in *those* and the unvoiced sound in *thing*? How do you know whether to make the voiced or unvoiced *th* sound in words such as *then, think, the* or *these*? The answer, of course, is that you know what sound to make when you know what the word is! But what are children to do if they are stuck on an unknown word, one that may be, or should be, in their speaking and listening vocabulary, but one they do not recognize on the page?

Asking readers to focus their attention on visual information frequently produces a condition that Frank Smith (1985) has aptly described as "tunnel vision." Since all they see are individual letters or parts of words, they can make little or no use of the non-visual information available to them. They are left trying to grunt and groan their way through the print and never *do* feel the syntactic and semantic flow or cohesion that should be present in the language of the story they are trying to read. They are so busy trying to remember the letter sounds they have already made that their memory system goes into overload. Not only are the sounds of those letters forgotten, but the content of the story also becomes blotted out. "Sounding out" cannot work effectively unless the reader has established control over the vast array of possibilities in the order of letters in a word, and their probable groupings, and knows instinctively when to use the strategy in conjunction with non-visual information.

Sound-it-out readers usually read in a slow, word-by-word manner (not to be confused with arhythmic reading) and pause for long periods of time on words they cannot recognize. They often say words that look and sound like what is on the page, but that do not make any sense. In their efforts to keep going, they may even produce non-words with the same characteristics. The reconstruction of meaning has been subjugated to the process of making sounds as the children try to read.

Examine carefully the following transcript of an 8-year-old (very bright!) boy as he tried to read part of a story he had already heard and read several times:

Text	Boy
Each picks a young tree. And each stands	Reach picks (pauses and starts again) . . . Reach picks and (self-corrects) . . . a young tree and reach stands
on its back legs and leans on its wide flat tail.	on the back lake (self-corrects) . . . black lake and leaves on its wind flat tail.

Some would say that he simply does not know his phonics. If he did, they would claim, he would never make all those stupid mistakes (we prefer to call them "miscues" now). But when you look at those miscues, you will see that nearly all of them look like and sound like what is on the page ("reach" for *each*; "black" for *back*; "lake" for *legs*; "leaves" for *leans*; "wind" for *wide*). In most cases (except "reach" for *each*), what he read even sounded like language. The trouble is, it did not make sense.

But this boy had never been asked to focus his attention on making sense while reading. From the time he entered school, he had been forced to look at the letters in words and sound them out. His program had been heavily phonics oriented, with a great deal of "oral circle reading" (reading aloud something new in front of peers who follow along in their books). Either focus alone would be almost certain to make him into a visually dependent reader — one who relies only on the print and gives no thought to whether what is being read makes sense. This boy knew all his phonics. What he did not know was how to make sense of what he was reading. Unfortunately, there are many children like him!

Helpful strategies

There are many positive suggestions parents and teachers can give when children are having problems. Often a simple, casual reference to the illustration will provide a meaningful clue. Or, sometimes drawing attention to a word with a similar pattern, one the children already know (*ball, wall,* etc.) will be enough.

The most important strategy to encourage is predicting what the word might be, based on what makes sense and what "sounds right." If their prediction meets these criteria and seems to match the available visual information, then they can continue. If it is a synonym substitution that does not match the visual information but that makes sense within the context of the story, they should be encouraged to read on, and be praised for their risk-taking. *Rerunning* — that is, returning to the beginning of the sentence to reread fluently — should be used in conjunction with predicting. If these strategies, alone or together, do not work, then rereading with the children might help. Gap-filling "cloze" strategies — pausing slightly just before the unknown word but supplying it if necessary, stretching it out — are often the most profitable ones.

If none of these strategies succeeds, then the children should be encouraged to leave the word out and read on. Frequently, they will find that when they reach the end of the sentence, the paragraph or the story, they can go back and fill the gap instinctively, experiencing a great deal of satisfaction when they do so.

Expanding horizons

At this fragile dependent/independent stage, the most important contribution parents and teachers can make to children's reading development is to provide quality reading materials. We cannot expect children to continue in their efforts to become independent readers with a diet of "stories" like *Sam. Sit Sam. Sam sits.*, found in one of the basal reading series still quite widely used. The idea persists that the "simpler" we make the language in children's first readers the easier it will be for them to read. Nothing could be further from the truth! Children learn to speak by hearing language that is complex, colorful and full of meaning. We do not drain the life, the variety and the meaning out of the spoken language we use in the presence of our children. Why, then, should we offer books that have been "simplified" until they are virtually impossible to read, with language of a kind children have never heard before, with stories so sterile and devoid of interest that children would never want to read them of their own volition? We insult their dignity and intelligence when we require them to read language of this kind.

Narrative text

The stories we provide for our children should be full of interest, with memorable and authentic language and with illustrations that match the story line in dynamic ways. Real authors do not produce the arid, vocabulary-controlled, phonically consistent language that litters the basal readers used in so many schools. The more predictable and natural the language and story patterns, no matter how complex and demanding, the easier the books will be for children to read. And most importantly, they will want to read them. There is no substitute for enjoyment. There is no substitute for books that stir the imagination. There is no substitute for quality, a characteristic readily availabe in so many of today's children's books.

I also advocate the use of series books at this stage of children's development. Mercer Mayer's series, starting with *Just for You*, and Gene Zion's *Harry* series are picture book examples. The Encyclopedia Brown, Hardy Boys and Nancy Drew stories are popular "chapter book" series. For years librarians in the United Kingdom tried to keep children away from Enid Blyton's stories, but they have always been read.

Why do these books, usually simple and repetitive in their plot, character development, resolution and so on, have such an appeal for children? It seems that, having read one or two, they are able to manage each succeeding one with little difficulty. The author's style becomes familiar and the language entirely predictable. The setting may change somewhat, but the characters, the story development and its resolution remain much the same. Each new title is read with more fluency as the children learn to orchestrate their use of the visual and non-visual cueing systems with little effort. Their control over narrative text is virtually complete.

Expository text

Once children have mastered the process of reading narrative text, they move quite naturally to learning expository forms. Their desire to know more about the world around them is strong. They want to learn about ballerinas, space exploration, horses, dinosaurs, how other people live. If expository text, as well as narrative, has been read to them on a reasonably regular basis, the move to reading this kind of material independently should be relatively painless. Expository text is usually more densely packed with new concepts and unfamiliar vocabulary, and the writing style is quite different. But books of this kind produced for children are usually very carefully written. They have a liberal supply of extremely supportive and explanatory illustrations. New concepts are introduced with plenty of clear explanation and a phonetic rendering of the vocabulary, if necessary, to aid both recognition and pronunciation.

Thematic studies are popular with both teachers and children. Children will read every available book on a topic that is of interest to them, and publishers are trying to meet this apparently irresistible urge. Witness, for example, the range of books, models, wall pictures and coloring books available about dinosaurs — the supply seems almost as inexhaustible as the children's interest. New topics to study are created by some exciting and wonderful nature programs on TV. Encyclopedic series such as *Childcraft — The How and Why Library* (Field Enterprises Education Corporation) and *The World Book Encyclopedia* (World Book Inc.) also provide rich and stimulating sources of information for children's ever-widening interests. Their appetites are limited only by the time they have available and their parents' and teachers' ability to provide the necessary materials, guidance and opportunities.

Poetry should continue to be shared with children as they develop as readers. The highly polished language of poems, with its intricate rhythms, subtle nuances and economic use of words, can grasp and hold their attention with surprising ease. And sometimes poetry can help them understand more clearly what is happening (and what might happen) in this confused and mixed-up world of ours. Children who are brought up with poetry as part of their literary experience will almost certainly want to read it (and probably write it) for themselves. They should have access to a variety of anthologies containing poems that touch on all walks and ways of life. Poems about the city, about the country, about fantasy and reality — all these and more should be read to, with and by the children. We must not allow the crafted and memorable language of poetry to lie idle and unread because we provide children with only a limited range of experiences with its various forms.

Conclusion

As children regain their earlier fluency, orchestrating visual and non-visual cueing systems, they need less and less help from those around them. There will still be times when an adult has to provide assistance because of the level of difficulty. But while too little assistance slows down growth, too much creates undue dependence.

Children who grow naturally as readers become readers. They consume print as an essential part of their daily diet. Just as they eat, breathe and drink to maintain their bodily functions, so readers go to books of all kinds to obtain essential nutrients for their minds. They know that what lies between the covers of books provides them with moments of relaxation, periods of intense stimulation, and flights of fantasy. Books provide access to an inexhaustible world of knowledge. Books become their constant companions. Through their reading, children grow in their ability to contribute in positive and useful ways to the society in which they live.

Epilogue: a child's right to literacy

I began this book with a look at two Lauras. The Laura Beths of this world have provided the raw data that led to the theories about literacy learning it describes. But it is for the Lauras of the world it was written.

Laura Beth found learning to read a relatively simple and extremely rewarding task. She learned without really knowing it. Her home experiences with written language of all kinds allowed her to grow into literacy as effortlessy and painlessly as she had grown into talking and listening. Her success as a reader and writer was assured.

Laura had different home experiences. She was not given the chance to grow into literacy naturally and entered school with a blind faith in her teachers' ability to teach her to read and write. But instead of finding it easy and enjoyable, she found it difficult and anxiety-producing. Her teachers concentrated on meaningless "reading readiness" skills and piecemeal language that failed to tap her already well developed language-learning strategies. Because she saw reading as "sounding out" letters and "saying" words, she continued to read in a halting, word-by-word way, without meaning or enjoyment.

Reading and writing must be learned the way they were meant to be learned: holistically. Before school, parents can contribute substantially to genuine literacy learning by immersing their children in a rich literacy-oriented environment. By listening to a wide variety of stories, poetry and expository text, children become thoroughly familiar with the structures and patterns of written language. Those who use it, and see it used around them, learn to recognize the importance of written language as a normal part of daily life. In school, teachers who accept responsibility for the literacy development of children must replace their old skills-oriented, teacher-dominated methodologies with holistically based strategies where control of what is being learned stays with the learner.

Many are doing just that, and implications for classroom practice are being spelled out to a growing audience of dedicated teachers through whole language conferences, professional books, articles in journals like NCTE's *Language Arts*, IRA's *The Reading Teacher* and CCTE's *Canadian Journal of English Language Arts*, and practical resource books like the *Whole Language Sourcebook* by Jane Baskwill and Paulette Whitman. Some teachers are also joining teacher-support groups to hear more about language and how it is learned. They talk about books and articles, share what they and their students are doing, discuss what works for them and what does not. They develop new strategies and examine new materials. Groups like TAWL (Teachers Applying Whole Language) espouse the principle of sharing: they learn from each other and from their students. Their professionalism is contagious and the positive results are beginning to be obvious. These teachers are becoming composers of their own literacy curricula rather than consumers of packaged commercial programs.

But teachers today have a second responsibility: they must also educate parents. In the past, they directed virtually all their attention to the children they were teaching, communicating only occasionally with parents in a newsletter or at a parent/teacher meeting. Now, they must give the parents their professional attention as well, to help them understand their role in the reading development of their children.

A group of teachers in Bridgewater, Nova Scotia, has produced a 15-minute slide/tape and a video presentation, both entitled *Project Baby Book*. In it they demonstrate, simply and graphically, why and how parents should read to their children from birth. Each mother in the district maternity home sees the presentation and receives a package containing some delightful children's books, explanatory pamphlets, a booklist and information about local library facilities. Fathers are encouraged to share the experience.

Jane Baskwill teaches in Lawrencetown, Nova Scotia. Parental misunderstanding of what she was trying to do in her whole language classroom led to a study exploring ways to educate and involve the parents. Her aim was to have them view themselves as partners in their children's education.

Early in the year, she provided each parent with a description of what she and the children did each day. At the first parent/teacher meetings, she showed slides of the children at work. She had invited whole families to come, and most of them did! Each month Jane sent a newsletter describing the current themes and how the parents might help, giving dates for upcoming trips, meetings and teacher inservice days, and summarizing the last parent/teacher meeting. The children took it home in a "Monthly Parent Bag," which also contained a book such as Marie Clay and Dorothy Butler's *Reading Begins at Home*, Bill Cosby's *Fatherhood* or Judith Newman's *The Craft of Children's Writing*. With each book she included a brief comment about something of interest and a card headed "What Do You Think?" Also included were brief notes to the parents about their children's development, and an invitation to write back and establish a "dialogue journal" with her. Many did. Once a week the children took home their own bag as well, with four or five suitable children's books to share or read alone. A booklet with suggestions for parents was usually included.

When the results of Baskwill's study are published, they will provide convincing evidence of the need for opening the channels of communication with parents so that home and school can form a true partnership in children's literacy development.

In literate societies, the most disempowered people are the illiterates, those who cannot read at all and those who turn away from books and print in frustration. We want our children to grow and feel confident that they are capable of making their own choices, of following their good sense, of knowing what they know and feeling good about it. We want them to develop an inner sense of power to control their own learning and direct their own lives. But we cannot expect this kind of confidence to develop in environments where control comes from others. The time has come for us to allow the task of learning to read and write to be based on natural language-learning needs that lie within the children themselves.

Children have rights. They have the right to literacy. They have the right to be assisted and guided in their learning. Whether they are highly proficient readers and writers like Laura Beth or "at risk" like Laura, they deserve nothing but the best from their parents and teachers. In order for these rights to be met, what is done to them in the name of literacy must not depart from the principles and practices that are the foundations of sound language learning. The ability to learn language, spoken and written, rests with our children. Let us provide the conditions in our homes and in our classrooms to allow it to flourish and blossom. The responsibility is ours. The future is theirs.

Bibliography

Baskwill, Jane. "Parents as partners," an unpublished Masters study. Acadia University, Wolfville, NS, 1987.

Baskwill, Jane and Paulette Whitman. *Whole Language Sourcebook*. Richmond Hill, Ont: Scholastic-TAB Publications, 1986.

Clay, Marie. *Reading: The Patterning of Complex Behavior*. Portsmouth, NH: Heinemann Educational Books, 1979.

Doake, David B. "Book experience and emergent reading behavior in preschool children," an unpublished Doctoral dissertation. University of Alberta, Edmonton, Alta, 1981.

Egan, Kieran. *Teaching as Story Telling*. London, Ont: The Althouse Press, 1986.

Elley, Warwick B. "ESL with ease, or, learning English painlessly through reading," from *Selected Proceedings of the 12th New Zealand Conference*. Christchurch: Canterbury Council of the International Reading Association, 1982.

Holdaway, Don. *The Foundations of Literacy*. Gosford, NSW: Ashton Scholastic, 1979.

Huey, Edmond R. *The Psychology and Pedagogy of Reading*. New York: Macmillan, 1908.

Iredell, Harriet. "Eleanor learns to read," in *Education*, Vol. XIX, No. 4, December, 1898. (Reprinted in *Language Arts*. Vol. 59, No. 7, 1982, pp.668-671).

Lenneberg, Eric H. *Biological Foundations of Language*. New York: Wiley and Sons, 1967.

Newman, Judith. *The Craft of Children's Writing*. Richmond Hill, Ont: Scholastic-TAB Publications, 1984.

Smith, Frank. *Essays into Literacy*. London: Heinemann Educational Books, 1983.

Smith, Frank. *Reading Without Nonsense*. New York: Teachers College Press, 1985.

Werner, Heinz. "The concept of development from a comparative and organismic point of view," in *The Concept of Development: An Issue in the Study of Human Behavior* by D. Harris. Minneapolis: The University of Minnesota Press, 1957.

The *Bright Idea* Series

In *Bright Idea* books, gifted authors reveal to readers the hearts of their professional lives. What has excited them professionally? What have they spent their years discovering, and why?

In these books they dress some old truths in new styles, and reveal some new truths about children, about language, about learning, about teachers, teaching and parenting.

The series was conceived and is published in Canada, but the authors come from all over: the United States, New Zealand, The Netherlands, Great Britain, Canada.

So far twelve titles have been published:

☞	**The Craft of Children's Writing**	Judith Newman
	Grand Conversations: **Literature Groups in Action**	Ralph Peterson and Maryann Eeds
	Learning Computer Learning	Veronica Buckley and Martin Lamb
	Other Countries, Other Schools	Mike Bruce
☞	**Reading Begins at Birth**	David B. Doake
☞	**Spel . . . Is a Four-Letter Word**	J. Richard Gentry
	Tests: Marked for Life?	S. Alan Cohen
	The Tone of Teaching	Max van Manen
☞	**What's Whole in Whole Language?**	Ken Goodman
	When School Is a Struggle	Curt Dudley-Marling
☞	**Whole Language: Inquiring Voices**	Dorothy Watson, Carolyn Burke and Jerome Harste
	A Word is a Word . . . Or Is It?	Michael Graves

In Canada, order from Scholastic Canada Ltd., 123 Newkirk Road, Richmond Hill, Ontario L4C 3G5.

In the United States, order from Scholastic Inc., P.O. Box 7502, Jefferson City, MO 65102.

☞ Available in New Zealand and Australia through Ashton Scholastic, and in the United Kingdom through Scholastic Publications.